Debating the War in Ukraine

Debating the War in Ukraine discusses whether the war could have been avoided and, if so, how? In this dialogical book, the authors discuss nodal points of history in terms of counterfactuals and contrastive explanations, concluding by considering future possibilities.

They start in the 1990s where several causal elements of the war originate involving Russia's economic developments and Europe's security arrangements. Moving on to the next decade, they focus on the Iraq war, colour revolutions, and NATO's 2008 announcement that Ukraine and Georgia will become members. Finally, they explore the past decade, including the Ukrainian crisis of 2013–2014, the annexation of Crimea, and the consecutive war in east Ukraine. The current war can also be seen as a continuum of that war. The authors agree that NATO's 2008 announcement on Ukraine's and Georgia's NATO membership was an unnecessary provocation, and that the implementation of the Minsk agreement could have prevented the current war, but otherwise their analysis of counterfactual possibilities differs, especially when it comes to the action-possibilities of the West (including diverse actors). These differences are not just dependent on different readings of relevant evidence but, importantly, stem from dissimilar contrast spaces and divergent theoretical understandings of the nature of states and mechanisms of international relations and political economy.

This short, highly accessible book will be of great interest to all those studying and working in international relations and its various subfields such as peace and conflict studies and security studies, as well as all those wishing to understand more about the backdrop of Russia's invasion of Ukraine in February 2022.

Tuomas Forsberg is Director of the Helsinki Collegium for Advanced Studies at the University of Helsinki, Finland, and Professor of International Relations at Tampere University, Finland.

Heikki Patomäki is Professor of World Politics at the University of Helsinki, Finland, and a Life Member of Clare Hall at the University of Cambridge, UK.

Debating the War in Ukraine
Counterfactual Histories and Future Possibilities

Tuomas Forsberg and Heikki Patomäki

LONDON AND NEW YORK

First published 2023
by Routledge
4 Park Square, Milton Park, Abingdon, Oxon OX14 4RN

and by Routledge
605 Third Avenue, New York, NY 10158

Routledge is an imprint of the Taylor & Francis Group, an informa business

© 2023 Tuomas Forsberg and Heikki Patomäki

The right of Tuomas Forsberg and Heikki Patomäki to be identified as authors of this work has been asserted in accordance with sections 77 and 78 of the Copyright, Designs and Patents Act 1988.

The Open Access version of this book, available at www.taylorfrancis.com, has been made available under a Creative Commons Attribution-Non Commercial-No Derivatives 4.0 license.

Trademark notice: Product or corporate names may be trademarks or registered trademarks, and are used only for identification and explanation without intent to infringe.

This book builds upon and updates 'Ukrainan sota: Dialogi historian kontrafaktuaaleista ja tulevaisuuden mahdollisuuksista' published in Finnish by *Kosmopolis* (Cosmopolis. Journal of Peace, Conflict and World Politics Research) Volume 52, Number 1, 2022. Reused under CC BY 4.0.

British Library Cataloguing-in-Publication Data
A catalogue record for this book is available from the British Library

ISBN: 978-1-032-45082-7 (hbk)
ISBN: 978-1-032-45086-5 (pbk)
ISBN: 978-1-003-37532-6 (ebk)

DOI: 10.4324/9781003375326

Typeset in Times New Roman
by Newgen Publishing UK

The Open Access version of this book was funded by University of Helsinki Library.

Contents

	Preface	vii
	Summary	ix
1	Introduction: On Explanations, Contrasts, and Counterfactuals	1
2	The 1990s: Sowing the Seeds of War After the End of the Cold War	7
3	The 2000s: Wars, Revolutions, and Misfired Declarations	21
4	The 2010s: The War in Ukraine Starts	31
5	2021–2022: Coercive Diplomacy and the Outbreak of War	46
6	The Shape of Things to Come	61
	Bibliography	80
	Index	92

Preface

On the day that Russia attacked Ukraine, 24 February 2022, we were at the gym and swimming as we do every now and then. We discussed the war and, above all, whether it could have been avoided and how. Over the years, we have had countless similar conversations. Although we have many joint interests, our theoretical research orientations as well as general political orientations are somewhat different. Typically, we agree on some things (for example basic metatheoretical foundations) and differ on others (for example various historical interpretations), but that is precisely what has made our discussions fruitful.

We originally wrote this piece in Finnish in March 2022 when the editor-in-chief of *Kosmopolis* magazine, Heino Nyyssönen, approached us individually with an invitation to write for a theme issue on the Ukrainian war. As we both consider that arguments have to be formed in relation to other, alternative interpretations, we thought that perhaps we could try the dialogue format. The history of this format is long. Early Plato (c. 437 BC – c. 347 BC) might have perfected the Socratic dialogue, but he had predecessors. Several well-known dialogues have been written by a single author, such as Berkeley or Hume in philosophy, and Johan Galtung in the social sciences. Although we are certainly not the first to employ dialogue in modern social sciences, the use of dialogue in this sense remains rather rare (see Griffiths 2015, however, for a debate book on the West's policy towards Russia), especially as ours is a dialogue between two real scholars – instead of imagined figures – agreeing and disagreeing on many things.

The original and considerably shorter text in Finnish was downloaded thousands of times from ResearchGate and the *Kosmopolis* website. A few colleagues made enquiries about a translation into English. In late spring 2022, our research assistant at the Helsinki Collegium for Advanced Studies, Matias Ingman, produced a preliminary draft translation of the text. As we started to update and polish the draft, we added a few points and new references here and there, and the text started to become longer. This raised the question of a suitable outlet for publication. Thus, in early July 2022, we approached Emily Ross from Routledge and asked whether our dialogue could be published in the *Focus* series, hoping to be able to contribute to the emerging first wave of the scholarly debate on Russia's invasion of Ukraine (see e.g. Dijkstra et al. 2022). We are grateful to the three anonymous referees for their excellent and very helpful comments; and to Emily for her support to the basic idea of this book.

Our shared starting point is that causal explanations must be located in real time and are thus necessarily historical. Hence, we structure our discussions chronologically in terms of decades from the 1990s to the 2020s and beyond. Through dialogue, we traverse some of the key nodal points of contemporary history and consider future possibilities from a broad world-historical perspective. The chronological approach does not mean that our explanations are linear in any sense or that we would see history as just "one damn thing after another". On the contrary, as our first methodological chapter indicates, we discuss social scientific explanations and employ technical terms such as causation, contrastive questions, counterfactuals, and minimal rewriting. This emphasis notwithstanding, the text is largely accessible and meant for a wide enlightened audience.

Apart from Heino Nyyssönen and Matias Ingman, we would like to thank several colleagues who have sent us feedback or encouraged us to develop our dialogue further, including Unto Vesa and Henri Vogt. Magnus Ryner has contributed to the development of the text by co-authoring with Heikki Patomäki a short article entitled "The EU's Role in the War in Ukraine". Tapio Kanninen and Haider A. Khan have discussed some of the key claims with Patomäki on several occasions and provided ideas. Forsberg would like to acknowledge the long-standing exchange of views with Graeme Herd. The usual disclaimer applies. Finally, we would like to express our gratitude to Lynn Nikkanen for her excellent work in editing the language of the final version.

Helsinki, 11 September 2022
Tuomas Forsberg and Heikki Patomäki

Summary

In this dialogue, we ask whether it is possible that the war in Ukraine could have been avoided and, if so, in what ways. The first chapter is methodological. We consider nodal points of history in terms of counterfactuals and contrastive explanations. We agree that "why?" and "what explains?" questions are contrastive and must be defined in terms of contrast spaces, although we do not necessarily agree on how to formulate those questions in the context of Ukraine. What exactly are the historical moments and situations where acting differently would have been a real possibility and could have had a major impact? Can we distinguish between proximate or immediate and ultimate or underlying causes of war? In what ways is history layered? The way we pose questions is also related to various pragmatic concerns and our positioning in social relations, and both involve normative considerations, for example in terms of responsibility.

In Chapter 2, we start our substantive discussions from the 1990s when several causal elements of the war were formed, including Russia's economic–political developments and Europe's post-Cold War security arrangements. Any starting point is, in a sense, arbitrary. It would be possible to frame the war in terms of a thousand-year struggle over Ukraine, the history of the capitalist world economy, the expansion of international society, the Cold War, or the effects of path dependence and cumulative causation through the Soviet era to present-day Russia. Our choice is based on the hypothesis that after the end of the Cold War and the collapse of the USSR, diverse paths were to an extent open. It is also important to be sufficiently specific about the relevant causal powers, mechanisms, and processes. Tuomas Forsberg (TF) focusses on (1) the development of the European security order and the role of NATO expansion within it; (2) the failure of democratisation in Russia; and (3) Vladimir Putin as a person and leader of Russia. Heikki Patomäki (HP) addresses these issues as well, while stressing the role of political economy, especially the disastrous effects of the so-called shock therapy. Some of our differences are related to NATO expansion – whether alternatives existed, whether promises were made, and so forth – but the discussion also moves on to deeper levels of social theory. A key theoretical question is whether state actors have ahistorical essences or whether the character of state actors is determined only or mainly by internal factors and processes (i.e. whether methodological nationalism is applicable). TF responds to HP's methodologically globalist critique by remarking that, "putting emphasis on the internal factors does not deny the potential or limited role of external factors and interaction".

In Chapter 3, we discuss the 2000s, focussing on the Iraq War, colour revolutions, and NATO's 2008 announcement that Ukraine and Georgia will become members. Putin rose to power in the autumn of 1999 and won the election the following summer. Facilitated by rising oil and gas prices in world markets, Putin's regime succeeded in reviving economic growth and stabilising society. During the brief cooperative spell of the early 2000s, there were even discussions about Russia's possible NATO membership. HP sees the invasion of Iraq that started in February 2003 as a world-historical nodal point, whereas TF stresses the importance of local developments and identifies the Orange Revolution from late November 2004 to January 2005 as the main turning point. Our interpretations of the colour revolutions differ somewhat in terms of allocating responsibility for various outcomes (TF blaming Putin's involvement, HP highlighting the inherent problems of the expansionary liberal projects of the US and the EU). We agree, however, that it was a mistake in 2008 to declare that NATO would expand to Georgia and Ukraine. What is more, this declaration occurred simultaneously with the deepening of the global financial crisis in 2008–2009. The crisis constituted another world-historical nodal point, paving the way for regressive developments involving the rise of nationalistic-authoritarian populism across the world. At the end of the chapter, we have the first round of debate about "whataboutism". TF accuses Russia of shifting the blame onto others, whereas HP maintains that double standards tend to erode international rules and principles.

Chapter 4 covers the 2010s and the start of the war in Ukraine. The nodal points of the 2010s include the Ukrainian crisis of 2013–2014, the annexation of Crimea, and the ensuing war in east Ukraine. The 2022 war can also be seen as a continuum from that war. Again, the key issue is whether internal developments or interactions in the context of the world economy and world time are decisive. For TF, the re-election of Putin in 2012 solidified the power of the clique that had been formed around the security services. Putinism started to be even more authoritarian. There were several anti-government protests in Russia in 2011–2013 in support of free elections, democracy, and civil rights, which did not lead to desirable outcomes and which were suppressed with the use of force and by restricting civil rights. "If Russia acts like this with regard to its domestic opposition, it makes the decision to wage war on other sovereign states more understandable". For TF, the onset of the war in Ukraine in early 2014 was also a result of interactions, but "the sin of the West was omission, while Russia's sin was commission". HP agrees with the depiction of developments inside Russia, but sees the internal/external dynamics as more complicated, also in Ukraine. Nationalist-authoritarian populism has risen in many countries across the world as a result of political economy developments, including in Russia and Ukraine; securitisation tends to mean de-democratisation; and the euro crisis and policies of austerity hit Ukraine in 2013, further instigating conflicts within Ukraine and between Russia and the West. At a more theoretical level, in this chapter, we deepen our discussions on "whataboutism" and methodological nationalism versus globalism. While some of these disagreements can be resolved by means of empirical research, others require argumentation about fundamentals (ontology, world-historical possibilities).

In Chapter 5, "2021–2022 Coercive Diplomacy and the Outbreak of War", we firstly ask: why did the conflict intensify during 2021? HP provides some possible explanations of timing in terms of Russia's positioning in the world economy, the build-up of Ukrainian military capabilities, and attempts to exert pressure on Russia to return Crimea to Ukraine. While TF dismisses these explanations, we agree that the decision-makers in Moscow were frustrated by the lack of progress in the implementation of the Minsk II agreement. This evokes a counterfactual according to which the implementation of Minsk II could have prevented the war. However, TF calls the idea of a neutral and "Finlandised" Ukraine flourishing between the EU and Russia a "realist delusion". HP does not agree that Minsk II would have meant the loss of Ukrainian sovereignty and subjugation to the control of Moscow (the autonomy of Donetsk and Luhansk would not have implied subjugation), but criticises TF for ignoring the importance of the question of NATO expansion. Our further discussions cover possible neo-imperial motives and their origins; the dangers of circular reasoning; the lack of good faith in negotiations; and the lack of willingness to negotiate. Amid divergent interpretations, we agree that there was something irrational about the way that Russian decision-makers disregarded the very high risks of the war. The discussions in Chapter 5 also involve theory, including new issues such as the certainty-of-hindsight bias, evaluative language, and the tasks of scholarship in the context of a violent conflict or war.

In the final chapter, we consider future possibilities and discuss the shape of things to come. TF argues that, given the absence of trust and decisive military success for either side, it is hard to see how a durable peace could be negotiated at the moment (in September 2022). Due to uncertainties and methodological difficulties, HP prefers to discuss the near future in normatively oriented terms by assessing the best- and worst-case scenarios, rather than in terms of prediction. For him, the best-case scenario concerns de-escalation and negotiated agreement capable of stopping the violence and destruction in Ukraine. It is not a matter of whether there will be an agreement, but rather when and on what terms. HP also briefly examines the worst-case scenario of escalation of the war, which seems more likely than the scenario of the war dragging on and becoming protracted – adding that the only rational course of action would be to work towards a world where the possibility of a nuclear war is zero. TF responds by criticising those Western scholars and pundits who suggest negotiations (1) for having little of substance to say about how such negotiations would restore a just or durable peace, and (2) for "Westsplaining", whereby the Ukrainians' own subjectivity is denounced. He refers to "the old wisdom", which holds that the conflict should firstly have reached some level of ripeness that has the characteristics of a "mutually hurting stalemate" before meaningful peace negotiations become possible. TF argues for strong military support for Ukraine as far as the additional risk of nuclear war remains small and for the containment of Russia. "Without a regime change in Russia, a new cooperative and rule-based security order cannot be rebuilt during the lifetime of our generation". HP counters by arguing that "ripeness" is a euphemism that masks the reality of war in Ukraine ("war is hell"). Any extra risk of a nuclear war is unacceptable. Finally, our discussion returns to the big picture of regressive developments in the dynamics of world economy and security. On a more positive note, the dialogue ends with a discussion on the relationship between the global security community and global reforms, and on the meaning of the recognition of equality in world politics. TF concludes his part by evoking the liberal idea of progress and the decline of violence.

1 Introduction
On Explanations, Contrasts, and Counterfactuals

HP: To start our discussion on whether the war in Ukraine could have been avoided, we should firstly outline the nature of contrastive questions and the meaning of counterfactuals, before proceeding to the discussion itself. The world is not deterministic. Causation is not about empirical regularities but about the production of effects in open systems that are susceptible to extrinsic influence and intrinsic change. Furthermore, societal causation occurs via agency, and reflective action involves the possibility of acting otherwise. From this point of view, it may be argued that any particular event – for example, war – could have been avoided, and not only in one but in many ways, because different actors can influence the outcome. On the other hand, there is a lot of continuity in the world and many aspects seem structurally or otherwise rather determined. Partly because of this, the common rule is that when we write historical counterfactuals, we should do it in a minimalistic manner, meaning that we should not stray far from the actual reality (Lebow 2010a, ch. 1). This principle can be problematic as well, but we should nonetheless understand how elements are connected and context-dependent. Only some things can be otherwise at any given time, and not everything is possible simultaneously.

In history, there are both periods of relative stability and critical nodal points, when specific turns of events and choices have an impact on which path the next phase of history will take (for the concept of nodal point, see Bhaskar 1986, 217 and Patomäki 2006, 9–18; for world-historical examples of counterfactual turning points, see Tetlock et al. 2006). A relevant question is: what exactly are the historical moments and situations where acting differently would have been a real possibility and could have had a major impact? Identification of key moments and critical junctures is not only an epistemological question but also concerns the logic of our questions (moreover, this kind of explanation involves considerations of ethical, political, and legal responsibility – aspects we return to later). The logic of questions concerns contrast spaces. Seemingly, the same question can have different meanings depending on the contrast spaces we imagine (see van Fraassen 1980; Garfinkel 1981; Morgan & Patomäki 2017). For example, a simple question such as "Why did Adam eat the apple?" (in the Bible or some other story) can be interpreted in many ways:

- Why did *Adam* eat the apple (instead of Eve eating it all by herself)?
- Why did Adam eat the *apple* instead of, say, a carrot or crisps?
- Why did Adam *eat* the apple and not make apple jam for his grandma, or throw it away?

Each contrastive why-question involves a set of possibilities, some of which are actual while others are counterfactual. The explication of possibilities can help to eliminate so-called hindsight bias (to be discussed later) and to question assumptions that are often taken for granted. Sometimes this questioning can have dramatic effects, especially when the focus is on decisive decisions or events in the context of war and peace. For example, Holger Herwig (2006) develops a counterfactual about World War II that is closely based on actual history and documents. In this scenario, Hitler wins in the East but dies in late summer 1945 because of deteriorating health and poisonous medical treatment. In autumn 1945, the US uses nuclear weapons against Germany, which capitulates in early 1946. This scenario could be criticised for downplaying the asymmetry of resources between the Axis and Alliance powers (in terms of population, GDP, and perhaps technology), but not all counterfactuals focus on decisions and events only. For instance, the contrastive question of "why did the Industrial Revolution occur in Europe in the early 19th century?" could be taken to mean:

- why did the Industrial Revolution occur *in Europe* in the early 19th century (rather than in China, the Islamic Arab world, or some other location)?
- why did the Industrial Revolution occur in Europe *in the early 19th century* (rather than some other time, earlier or later)?

By combining the two questions, we can ask questions specifying alternative locations and times. For instance, many scholars argue that the 11th–12th century Song China the first "modern" economy that was not only "proto-capitalist" but also close to, and had potential for, an industrial revolution. Answers to these kinds of contrastive questions tend to involve slow processes (for example collective learning in the field of metallurgy) and social structures (for example large-scale hierarchical empires of the military-agrarian era tended to prevent or at least slow down institutional and technological experimentation, including occasional periods of regress or even collapse).

Finally, it must be stressed that the way we pose questions is related to pragmatics and our positioning in social relations. For example, if a person dies in a car crash, a police officer, a doctor, an engineer, and a traffic planner can all offer explanations for the outcome. All of these have different contrast spaces in their mind (e.g. Has there been a violation of traffic laws and, if so, how?; What was the physiological cause of death?). Explanations can be compiled, and this is something a good social scientist must always try to accomplish; and yet there are many pragmatic interests, contrast spaces, and values behind any such compilation. This is definitely true also for counterfactuals concerning the current war in Ukraine.

TF: Could the full-scale war in Ukraine that began in 2022 have been avoided? The question of how wars can be avoided is at the heart of both peace research and the whole discipline of International Relations. This is why there is ample research on the causes of war, concerning both specific wars and wars in general. However, an approach relying on explicit counterfactuals has long been shunned in this literature, even though in principle it is ingrained in all causal explanations (e.g. Levy 2015). Distinguishing between proximate or immediate and ultimate or underlying causes of war is commonplace.[1] Sometimes a more multi-layered taxonomy of proximate, intermediate, and underlying reasons can be applied. In these schemes, proximate causes can be highly contingent and – counterfactually – their removal would not have prevented the war as it would most likely have started for other proximate reasons. A counterfactual argument about the possibilities of avoiding a war is most powerful when it deals with a cause that is significant and contingent at the same time – a necessary part of the causal complex and difficult to replace with another cause without a major rewriting of history, but which is there for some random reasons.

Scholarship on the causes of World War I could fill dozens of bookshelves (see e.g. Levy & Vasquez 2014). The war has become particularly interesting from the point of view of counterfactual analysis, as none of the many causes of the war was so prominent that it could be regarded as sufficient for the outbreak of the war. The war can therefore be understood as an aggregate effect of a number of contingent causes, like the assassination of Archduke Franz Ferdinand, which materialised simultaneously within a short time window (Lebow 2014;

also 2010a). The developments that led to World War I has been seen as analogous to the war in Ukraine, particularly through the metaphor of "sleepwalking" (Clark 2013; Walt 2022).[2]

On the other hand, World War II has also offered analogies to the war in Ukraine. The most (stereo)typical analogy is that Russia is likened to Germany and Putin to Hitler. German militarism and fascism are seen as the ultimate causes of World War II, which again resulted from the experienced humiliation caused by the Versailles peace treaty, and from the Great Depression, enabling Hitler's rise to power. Proximate causes, like the Munich agreement or the Molotov–Ribbentrop pact just before the war, were therefore not crucial for the war because the ultimate causes were so significant. In this analogy, the end of the Cold War and the economic turmoil in the 1990s form the respective Russian experiences of humiliation, paving the way for Russian nationalism and Putin's rule. Moreover, the analogy to the 1939–1940 Winter War between the Soviet Union and Finland has also been prevalent, understood as an unprovoked war by Russia against a weaker but peaceful neighbour.

Frank Harvey's (2013) book on the Iraq War could be mentioned here as a relatively recent counterfactual analysis of the causes of war. As it is easy to argue that George W. Bush's presidential victory was highly contingent (upon only a few hundred votes in Florida), it is worth asking what if the result had been different. If Al Gore had been elected president, would he have started the war? Somewhat controversially, as the war is typically seen as Bush's war, Harvey concludes that the US would have waged war in Iraq after the 9/11 attacks even with Al Gore as president.

As a counterfactual analysis cannot examine every possible moment and situation, we have to choose some events that are either theoretically relevant or deemed important in the ongoing discussion (on contrastive explanations of Russian foreign policy, see Forsberg 2019). We can try to articulate some justified critical junctures that we find crucial and that have influenced the development of the situation in a notable manner. There is undoubtedly a strong subjective element in creating counterfactuals and drawing consequences from them (see Tetlock and Visser 2000 precisely in relation to assessments of Russia). Ethical considerations in choosing a contrast must be remembered, too: when some aspects are selected as variables, others are considered normal. Alan Garfinkel (1981, 141) gives an example of a fighting couple: if the wife is asked what she did that started the fight, the cause of the fight is being seen as attributable to the wife instead of the husband. Similarly, we can ask what did Ukraine do to induce Russia to wage the war, but then the contrast is why Russia attacked Ukraine (and not Kazakhstan, for example), or why Russia attacked Ukraine in 2022 (and not in 2021), and not the question of why did Russia attack Ukraine at all (rather than sticking to peaceful diplomacy).

One way of going through various counterfactual possibilities related to the Ukraine War is to analyse them chronologically. We could discuss the aftermath of the fall of the Soviet Union first, and continue to the rise of Putin, then move to the 2000s, which include the colour revolutions, and the famous NATO declaration of 2008 that Georgia and Ukraine will join NATO. After this, we can ponder the 2010s, focusing on the Ukraine crisis of 2013–2014, the annexation of Crimea, and the ensuing war in east Ukraine. Then we could discuss the developments that took place just before the war, and finally say something about the future. In a contrastive manner, we can ponder whether the war would have erupted at all, or whether it would have just been a "special military operation" rather than a full-scale war.

HP: These are excellent points raising many further important questions, which we could discuss at length. Instead of "ultimate causes",[3] I prefer to talk about geohistorical layers and would also distinguish between causes related to (1) agency, and (2) structure and mechanisms. Both are involved in a causal complex. The first goal is to explain the formation of agency and its positioning in social practices and relations. Everything is historical and so actors and their agency are context-bound, as are social structures and mechanisms. Even in periods of relative stability, actors are in a state of (potential) change. Types of agency or structures can disappear – or be absented – from a given scene. For example, the causes of World War I formed a complicated complex, the elements of which can be traced back to different layers of history (see Patomäki 2008, ch. 4 and app. 2). Still, World War I was not inevitable. In my assessment, if the crisis of summer 1914 had been resolved diplomatically (like the Moroccan crisis of 1911), the probability of avoiding a major war in the 1910s would have been 0.5. Events already unravelling at that time would have removed at least some of the causes of the war by the 1920s (this would not have removed the possibility of a great-power war as such; in his 1913–1914 book *The World Set Free*, H.G. Wells anticipated a nuclear war in the mid-20th century, in some ways quite correctly). World history could have evolved in a different way.

Another subject for lengthy discussion could be the role of analogies and narratives in the constitution of agency and the reasoning of actors. Consider how Ukraine and NATO expansion are seen in Russia as being related to World War II. Whereas several countries of the former

Eastern Bloc are seeking NATO protection against Russia, reminiscent of the repressive Soviet era of 1945–1989, in Russia it has been equally common to evoke memories of how East European states from Finland to Bulgaria joined the Axis in 1940–1941. All historical analogies distort reality and can also be dangerous in terms of aggravating current hostilities. Epistemologically, our problem as researchers concerns how to recognise similar horizontal (events) and vertical (processes and structures) relations in a reasonable manner, given that even the best analogies are only partial. And, more generally, to what extent can we lean on historical analogies? (Patomäki 2017, 812–813).

However, I will stop my methodological reflections here so that our discussion does not meander too much. Let us turn our attention now to the developments that are directly relevant in explaining the current war in Ukraine.

Notes

1 This distinction is often seen as one already made by Thucydides (1972, I.1.23) in his *Peloponnesian War*, where he lists several immediate causes of the war but thinks that the real cause is Sparta's fear of Athenian hegemony.
2 Christopher Clark himself, however, thinks that the 1914 analogy is flawed as the case of Russia's invasion of Ukraine is not as complex as the run-up to World War I: "it's quite clearly a case of the breach of the peace by just one power" (Oltermann 2022).
3 This question also concerns the interpretation of Thucydides (cf. ch. 7 of Patomäki 2002). Thucydides made a distinction between *aitia* and *prophasis*. Edmunds (1975, 172–173) argues that, for Thucydides, *prophasis* meant "true cause" or perhaps even "ultimate cause" (my own 2002 discussion on p. 179 based one-sidedly on Edmunds was a bit confusing). A rather different reading would be more in line with the notion that, in essence, *The History of the Peloponnesian War* is a moralist tragedy written in conformity with the conventions of its own time and context (Patomäki 2002, 188–189). In this reading, *aitia* and *prophasis* are primarily normative and evaluative concepts. *Aitia* could be translated as "accusation", "complaint", "grievance", while the corresponding passive means "guilt", "blame", or "responsibility". In turn, *prophasis* can be translated as "excuse" or "pretext", that is, understood in terms of rationalisation (Pearson 1952, 205–208; also Pearson 1972). In other words, the underlying complaints and grievances, or alternatively the true reasons for a course of action, may be different from its contemporary or later rationalisations.

2 The 1990s

Sowing the Seeds of War After the End of the Cold War

TF: The discussions on the root causes of the Ukraine war usually start from the 1990s, focusing on the end of the Cold War and its aftermath. How is it possible that, despite all the widespread optimism that reigned back then, we have ended up with a destructive full-scale war in Europe? The discussion has revolved around three issues: (1) the development of the European security order and the role of NATO expansion within it; (2) the failure of democratisation in Russia; and (3) Putin as a person and leader of Russia. These categories reflect the levels of analysis outlined by Kenneth Waltz (1959): the international system, the state, and the individual.

It is obvious by now that the construction of a common European security order failed in the 1990s. But what would have been a realistic alternative? The OSCE-based system that Russia cherished would have been too weak to prevent the war. Russia also started to treat the OSCE with scepticism by the end of the 1990s. The perceived threat of NATO expansion is easy to cite as a proximate cause of the Ukraine War, but could we have avoided the war if NATO had not expanded at all (see Marten 2017)? Would the war be waged then in the Baltic states or Poland instead if Russia's development had been what it has been? The enlargement of NATO can be seen as a meaningful counterfactual because it was not inevitable, at least not in the mid-1990s. The idea was contested and it did not have widespread support in Washington to begin with. Yet the desire of the former people's democracies in East Central Europe to join NATO did not wane that easily, and the pressure for expansion would have remained had President Clinton not adopted the pro-enlargement policy.

A central question has been the alleged broken promises that the West made to Russia about not enlarging NATO. It is not only Putin who appealed to these promises in the negotiations before the war when wanting a binding agreement from NATO that it would not expand, but also several Western scholars and pundits, who have emphasised that such broken promises had fostered mistrust and bitterness in Russia (Shifrison 2016; Sarotte 2021). This story is problematic both normatively and causally when considering whether such binding promises were made on the one hand, and whether the idea of given promises, whether justified or not, actually mattered.

First, the so-called promises were mostly singular oral statements, like the famous "not one inch eastwards" guarantee given by US Secretary of State James Baker, which was given before the unification of Germany and concerned East Germany in that context (see Kramer 2009; Sarotte 2021). These assurances were given to Mikhail Gorbachev in a very different era of a prevailing Cold War, and not to Russia and its leaders Boris Yeltsin or Vladimir Putin after the collapse of the Soviet Union. The assurances were given in the course of negotiations and not as a joint deal, with the exception of the 2+4 negotiations concerning Germany, but the treaty did not focus on the wider security arrangements in Europe and did not mention NATO. Instead, the Soviet Union and its successor Russia had underlined several times since the Paris document of 1990 that a key principle of the European security architecture is that sovereign states are free to choose their own security arrangements, and whether they choose to join alliances or not.[1] This was thought to be consistent with the idea that Europe is whole and free.

Furthermore, it is worth noting that the idea that the West gave and broke promises with regard to NATO enlargement, irrespective of whether they were real or not, was not a prevalent issue in Russia in the 1990s. The allegations that the West had broken promises became an important part of the Russian victimisation story and bitterness in the 2000s, as the relationship with the West started to cool. Although NATO expansion was widely criticised in Russia, and regarded as a bad idea for a variety of reasons, arguments about Western promises seldom surfaced in the public discussion (see Sergounin 1997). Yeltsin did bring up the 2+4 agreement about German unification, but this attempt did not really fly. In addition, both Yeltsin and Putin accepted, albeit reluctantly, that NATO expansion was a fact that could be lived with. When visiting Helsinki in September 2001, Putin said that NATO expansion to the Baltics should not be treated hysterically – and that Russia was even ready to discuss its own membership of the Alliance (see Forsberg & Herd 2015). NATO's door was never formally closed to Russia, but the problem was that it was not given special treatment in the application procedure.

Of course it can be claimed that the West could have taken Russia's concerns and viewpoints into greater consideration, and thereby affirmed Russia's national self-esteem in a healthy manner (Hill 2018). For example, NATO's partnership programme was first marketed as an alternative to NATO membership, but it soon became the first step towards NATO enlargement (Goldgeier 2019). In particular, the Kosovo War in 1999 – maybe even more than NATO enlargement – consolidated the Russian perception that the US and NATO have a hegemonic position in the European security order and that they can use military power without Russian approval, namely illegally without a UN Security Council mandate if they so wish (see Marten 2017).

However, it is not true that the West did not take Russia's interests into account at all, or that it was excluded completely. The "Russia first" policy largely prevailed when it came to the former Soviet Union. Russia's military activity in the former Soviet Union, like "peacekeeping" in Georgia and Tajikistan, was seen as a stabilising element, largely tolerated in the West and only nominally criticised, as in the case of Transnistria (see Chayes et al. 1997). Russia was a party to the Budapest Memorandum of 1994, stipulating that Ukraine will forgo its nuclear weapons in exchange for security guarantees on its territorial sovereignty. Counterfactually, it can be asked whether there would be a war if Ukraine had remained a nuclear state, a viewpoint that John Mearsheimer (1993), for example, supported. Russia was also a member of the Contact Group on the former Yugoslavia together with the US and other European great powers, even though its policies were mostly drawn up by the US. With the Contact Group, Russia had agreed to demand a ceasefire, the withdrawal of Yugoslav and Serbian forces from Kosovo, the return of refugees, and unlimited access for international monitors before the war, and it was part of the diplomatic solution to end the war as well as the post-conflict stabilisation process. Russia was also admitted to the G-7, the summit for advanced industrialised nations, even though it was not eligible to belong to this group according to the economic criteria.

For Russia, the core priorities were in the former area of the Soviet Union rather than in influencing the European security order or global politics as a whole. Here, the basic problem was something that was not properly addressed in any political framework after the end of the Cold War, namely the issue of peaceful territorial change (which we discussed as early as the 1990s; see Forsberg 1995). Russia was not fully satisfied with its borders after the collapse of the Soviet Union, but the territorial integrity of sovereign states was a core pillar of the Cold War security system that was bequeathed to the post-Cold War era. It was a robust principle that protected all states equally, but at the same time it was very rigid when it came to disintegrating states such as the Soviet Union and Yugoslavia. It would have been very difficult for the West to rediscuss and reform the principles of territorial changes and, as a matter fact, Russia itself did not want to open the issue either as it also faced some actual or potential territorial claims from its neighbours.

A separate, but not completely distinct question is whether the West could have done more to further strengthen the democratisation in Russia in the 1990s (Deudney & Ikenberry 2021). The counterfactual assumption here is that a democratic Russia would not have ended up waging war in Ukraine, as democracies do not wage war with each other. Discussion on this question has been carried out under the heading "Who lost Russia?" (e.g. Conradi 2017). This discussion typically concludes that much could have been done better, but in the end the development was a result of Russia's domestic factors, which were difficult to influence from outside. The democratic tradition in Russia was weak and even liberal-minded politicians who believed in democratic institutions were not capable of cooperation, and ended up fighting each other (see Gelman 2015). The constitutional crisis of 1993 – that is, before any serious debate about NATO enlargement in the West – already indicated that things had started to turn sour, even though several features of a liberal-democratic state, such as elections, pluralistic mass media, and freedom of opinion and assembly, were still intact.

In this context, Russia's economic development is yet another issue. The internal chaos in Russia, widening income inequalities, and the rouble's collapse in the late 1990s affected Russia's self-esteem and strengthened the narrative of humiliation. Moreover, personal experiences related to shortages and a decline in living standards may often have been more humiliating than the treatment of the Russian state. These factors explain the rise of Putin at the end of the 1990s and his continued widespread popularity, but several nations and states have faced similar hardship without engaging in military aggression.

Indeed, the whole issue of Russia's humiliation in the 1990s should receive more systematic attention. It has become a narrative that is widely accepted as a given without any thorough empirical evidence based on perceptions and experiences. At a general level, as Russians' felt experience of their reduced status, it is easy to accept, but its actual causes are not that self-evident. In my view, the West tried to avoid humiliating Russia by treating it as a great power, but it did not regard Russia as a superpower equal to the US (for the British attitude, see Horovitz 2021). A prime example of humiliation concerned the Kosovo War: Russia may have felt humiliated by the fact that it could not veto something that all the other great powers in the Contact Group supported, but the more humiliating aspect of the war was undoubtedly Russia's own failed military intervention. Moreover, some manifestations of Russia's humiliation, such as Russian President Boris Yeltsin being drunk during his state visits, were more self-inflicted than imposed.

It is a paradox that the felt humiliation led Russia to search for pride in its great-power past, but policies carried out on the basis of such great-power identity were likely to lead to new humiliating experiences because they were out of touch with the prevailing international practice (see Neumann and Pouliot 2011). Indeed, one of the problems in Russia was that there was never a proper attempt to come to terms with the past after the break-up of the Soviet Union. The Soviet-era atrocities were not systematically accounted for, and the position of the KGB was not critically examined. The fall of the Soviet Union, new borders, and the diaspora of millions of Russians outside of Russia's state borders were never fully accepted. Russia's identity as a great power, if not an empire, rested on a past legacy that became a major source of pride. Its relationship with an independent Ukraine has been a sore point ever since the 1990s (see Lester 1994). According to the famous assessment by Zbigniew Brzezisnki (1997, 49), Ukraine was not only geopolitically important but an essential part of Russia's identity as an Eurasian empire.

Finally, we can ask what part Putin, as the leader of Russia, has played in steering Russia's course to the war. If someone other than Putin had become the president of Russia, could the war against Ukraine have been averted? As Putin was not the obvious successor to Yeltsin, there was ample room for contingency. It was clear from the outset, however, that there was great demand in Russia for a nationalistic leader, who would very likely have authoritarian tendencies and shun Western cooperation. General Alexander Lebed, for example, could have been one possible alternative, but he perished in a helicopter accident. Putin's KGB background and the cynicism instilled in it, deep mistrust towards outsiders, a tendency to bend the rules, and to lie blatantly if necessary in order to achieve strategic goals, have been seen as factors that are characteristic of Putin and that can account for Russia's decision to attack Ukraine. Putin's operational code was based on principles that did not shy away from using military force, but he appeared more of an opportunist than a strategist (Dyson & Parent 2018). As Putin himself recounted, he learned from the streets of Leningrad that if a fight seems inevitable, it is better to strike first (see Putin 2015).

Putin nevertheless began his first presidential term in the early 2000s by cooperating with the West. In hindsight, this seems instrumental, but we cannot exclude the possibility that he was genuine in his attempt to get closer to the West, although the policy failed. By the mid-2000s, Putin started to get frustrated and bitter in his public speeches and meetings with Western leaders. An antagonistic relationship with the West, however, would not have automatically led to the war on Ukraine. At least to some extent, the Ukraine war was "Putin's war". Even though the annexation of the Crimean peninsula was greeted with wide acceptance among the population, many patriotic and NATO-sceptical retired soldiers like Colonel-General Leonid Ivashov criticised the launch of a full-scale war. Why Russia started the large-scale war in Ukraine during Putin's term might be down to Putin's idiosyncratic personality traits, such as a strong tendency to despise and punish those who do not submit to his will, particularly if they are weaker (Pursiainen & Forsberg 2021, 278–282). On the other hand, it is possible that the long reign and corruption also affected Putin's personality by strengthening the elements of paranoia, bitterness, and power syndrome. However, this is not something that can be related to the 1990s.

HP: Thank you for the comprehensive overview of the most relevant counterfactuals of the 1990s. I am particularly delighted that you mentioned the economic (mal)developments of Russia as I tend to think that political economy processes have been central to how forms of agency and actors – positioned in practices and relations of power – have developed in and through Russia. These processes, in part, explain why those constructing the post-Cold War Russian identity started quite early on to distance themselves from the prevalent Western story. Unfavourable economic development was a primary reason for the collapse of the Soviet Union. From 1928 to 1970, the USSR did not grow as fast as Japan, but was arguably the second most successful economy in the world. Robert C. Allen (2001) reasons that the main causes of the decline in growth after 1970 were disastrous investment decisions, especially the increasingly impairing over- and mis-investment in capital goods and heavy industry, and the diversion of research and development resources to the military. The main aim of *perestroika* and *glasnost* was to respond to the problems of the Soviet economy. Gorbachev and his government did not, however, have a systematic plan for resolving the economic problems. While Gorbachev's economic reforms increased the profits of a few companies, they diminished the financial base of the state and led to progressively deeper regression. The situation was exacerbated by falling oil prices and decreasing oil production. By 1991, central power was losing or had already lost its control over the economy, and its solvency was questioned (Mazat 2016).

The West had turned to neoliberalism (for a conceptual and political history of neoliberalism, see Patomäki 2021, esp. 104–109, 114–123) with the leadership of Margaret Thatcher and Ronald Reagan, and interpreted the end of the Cold War as "the victory of the free West". Neoliberals took the economic troubles of the Soviet Union as a further demonstration that only "free markets" work. The idea was that Russia could be treated with "shock therapy" (a comparison with China's development could give us plenty of material for an interesting counterfactual that could have involved the continuation of the USSR; cf. Weber 2021). The term "shock therapy" is a metaphor that originates from 1970s psychotherapy, where mental illnesses were treated by administering chemical or electric shocks to the patient. Ultimately, the shock therapy of the 1990s was based on ignorance about Russian society. The idea was to destroy the old, with the assumption that a new utopian market system would replace it. Against the expectation of experts such as Jeffrey Sachs, shock therapy led to a disaster that included two hyperinflation periods, the downfall of industrial production, and skyrocketing inequalities (Mareeva 2020; Sachs later criticised the shock therapy and complained that some of his advice, such as establishing a stabilisation fund or cancelling part of Russia's debts, were not followed: Goodman 2022). A group of former state managers and black marketeers managed to amass massive wealth by privatising collective property – duly becoming "oligarchs". The power of organised crime also increased in the 1990s, which likewise played its part in producing new super-rich individuals.

These changes led to a significant drop in the living standards of average Russians. The changes brought about mass poverty even among well-educated and trained workers. By the beginning of the 1990s, a third of Russians had already fallen below the poverty line and, by the end of the decade, the ratio was almost 40% (during the late Soviet era, it was only 2%, although the circumstances were different). If we want to understand the effects of shock therapy, we need a theory of the capitalist market economy that recognises the role of structures and institutions and can analyse cumulative causation, self-reinforcing processes, and positive feedback loops. Politely put, mainstream economics did not live up to its promises. The failure of shock therapy was no surprise from the perspective of institutionalist, post-Keynesian, or Marxian economics – and it was no surprise even for a new Keynesian like Joseph Stiglitz (2003), who relies on mainstream methods.

The chaotic 1990s gave way to a countermovement. By the end of the decade, most Russian experts, politicians, and ideologues that I knew or interviewed at the time wished for a strong and, if necessary, authoritarian leader within a somewhat liberal framework that could constrain the oligarchs, even partly, and successfully manage a form of state-led capitalism. Civil society, at the time, was filled with a plethora of diverse ideas.[2] Even though interests and meanings offered by the West and presented as universal were quite widely accepted in Russia at the beginning of the 1990s, the politico-economic repercussions of the failed shock therapy led to re-evaluation and reassessment in the context of a sense of humiliation, as you pointed out. At the same time, the tendency of the US and some of the EU member states to use military force to advance their interests and intentions, often disregarding international law, reinforced this development.

There were alternatives to shock therapy. Apart from China (Weber 2021), the developments in the Czech Republic, Poland, and Slovenia have differed significantly from the Russian experience as they have managed to keep inequality under control after their surge in the early 1990s (in the early 2020s, their inequality levels are comparable to that of neoliberalised Finland), and in general socio-economic developments have been relatively favourable (also because the concentration of European industrial production around Germany has benefitted them). On the other hand, we might ask whether there was something in the context of the early 1990s – characterised by a belief in the end of history, the triumph of the West, neoliberal hegemony, and globalisation – that made acting otherwise unlikely, or even impossible. The overall direction seems to have been the same almost everywhere (see for example Harvey 2005; also Patomäki 2008, ch. 6), even though there were plenty of dissidents in most contexts (including this author). Hegemony belonged to the likes of Yeltsin, who believed in the blessings of radical liberalisation and privatisation. What is equally noteworthy is that the collapse of the Soviet Union "shrank the imaginative and ideological space in which opposition to capitalist thought and practices might incubate", with far-reaching political consequences also in the West, including the US. This strengthened and consolidated the neoliberal order across the world (Gerstle 2022, ch. 5, quotation p. 149).

Concurrent with the implementation of shock therapy, the political leaders devised post-Cold War security arrangements in Europe and also globally. "Security" is not only about the protection of people's lives, but typically includes the preservation of possessions and power relations, some normative principles (for example adhering to promises and agreements), and fundamental perspectives on one's historical existence (who are we, where do we come from, where are we going?). Security could have been organised collectively. I agree, however, that OSCE- and UN-based systems are incapable of preventing wars started or waged by the great powers. This is because both, and especially the UN, have been designed so that the UK, China, France, Russia, and the US can prevent decisions with their veto (for a critique of the UN veto powers in the context of Ukraine, see Chowdhury 2022). Yet the point is somewhat off the mark. The question is not whether the OSCE could *prevent* a military attack by military or related means, but rather whether reliance on the OSCE could have led to a more cooperative security order in Europe.

Instead of developing the OSCE or the UN, NATO expanded, and this has affected the positioning of Russia in world politics and contributed to the creation of contemporary Russian identity and agency. At the beginning of Putin's term in 2000–2001, there were still discussions about Russia's NATO membership, but Putin's hesitant proposals for equality with the US were met with a lukewarm reception. Russia has a privileged position in the UN, and has been recognised in the OSCE as an equal member, whereas in NATO the US has the leading position. Moreover, it is clear that several former members of the Eastern Bloc have sought security through NATO *against* Russia. The NATO-centred order excludes Russia and is somewhat posited against it (the wider context includes the nuclear deterrence that Russia inherited from the USSR and that was targeted against the US). The expansion of NATO had an unintended negative altercasting effect (cf. Wendt 1999, 76, 129, 329, 346), which in turn has shaped the redefinition of Russia's identity and position.

You write that "the enlargement of NATO [...] was not inevitable, at least not in the mid-1990s [...as] it did not have widespread support in Washington". I agree in some ways. It would have been possible to choose the development of common institutions, instead of US- and NATO-centred security arrangements and their one-sidedness. Yet there are some presuppositions in the rhetorical questions that you pose that I do not agree with, for example:

> The OSCE-based system that Russia cherished would have been too weak to prevent the war. Russia also started to treat the OSCE with scepticism by the end of the 1990s. The perceived threat of NATO expansion is easy to cite as a proximate cause of the Ukraine War, but could we have avoided the war if NATO had not expanded at all?

I might answer your last question in the affirmative. You seem to assume that there is a given essence, nature, or internal tendency in Russia to develop in an aggressive and repressive direction, independently of the development of relevant social contexts and processes. I do not support this sort of essentialism.[3] Although I tend to agree with Hannah Arendt (1958) that actors in a sense "reveal" their nature via their actions, the temporary essence of actors is a result of processes and a product that itself changes via processes and actions. From an ontological perspective, identities, preferences and the like are not only "revealed" but also constructed through inter- and intra-actions and, as such, they are sensitive to framing and context effects, for example. In the constant process of structuration, there is of course no such moment when actors are *tabula rasa* in the sense of being receptive to any (re)constitution. What we are seeing are processes of structuration in which various layers of history are present, many processes are path-dependent, and causation tends to be cumulative.[4] For example, Putin as a person represents some continuation from the late Soviet Union and its security police, although his background is also rooted in the democratic politics of the 1990s, and so forth.

One question you raise is whether the Soviet leadership was promised during the end of the Cold War and German unification that NATO would not expand toward Russia's borders. You write that "this story is problematic both normatively and causally", and emphasise that in the 1990s NATO expansion was not a central question in Russia. Every episode in history is up for interpretation and suspect to reinterpretation, and this is no exception. Every reinterpretation is a result of changing contexts and is part of reforming societal relations and positions. It is obvious that during German unification NATO expansion was not on the agenda (unification happened in October 1990, and the Warsaw Pact was not officially dismantled until summer 1991). The EU said no to a possible Russian membership in 1994.[5] Since that point, EU–Russia relations have been *external*. By 1994, the *momentum* for Western (neo) liberalism started to dwindle in Russia. However, there may have been less need to emphasise broken promises as long as Russian politicians wanted to develop cooperation with NATO, or even apply for membership, although this is complicated as even Yeltsin consistently used words such as "humiliation" and "fraud" to describe plans to extend NATO to the countries of eastern (central) Europe. For example, at the OSCE conference in Budapest in December 1994, plans to expand NATO provoked a public outburst from Yeltsin (National Security Archive 2021). The alienation between political communities deepened in the early 2000s when Russia started to distance itself more systematically from the allegedly universal values of the West and its interests and intentions.

What is the historical truth concerning promises not to expand NATO? Some of the actors involved, like Eduard Shevardnadze, have later denied the existence of any promise, while some disagree with Shevardnadze completely. For instance, in his memoirs William Burns (2019, 55–56), who attended these discussions as a diplomat and in 2021 became the director of CIA, recalls that the Soviets were reassured that after German unification NATO would not be extended any farther to the east. According to a meticulous analysis made by *Der Spiegel* (Klußmann et al. 2009), there is no doubt that Western leaders did everything they could to give the impression that NATO membership was out of the question for countries like Poland, Hungary, and Czechoslovakia. The impression is not the same as an unambiguous public promise or written agreement, but the story of the promise not to expand is not baseless. Moreover, from the viewpoint of Russia, NATO expansion reveals the nature of Western actors. This has often been interpreted in Russia via a particular (misleading) historical analogy to Operation Barbarossa, which ultimately led to the death of some 30 million Soviet citizens. Essentialism like this is dangerous (see note 3).

To sum up, according to my interpretation of the 1990s, there are many situations in which the US, the Western alliance, and the EU (which evolved into its current form in 1992) could have acted differently towards Russia. The economic developments of the late Soviet Union were in many ways intrinsic, but they also reflected changes in the world time and changes in the global economy.[6] Even though it is true that Boris Yeltsin's government adopted shock therapy, this adoption was also dependent on conditionalities set by the West and the IMF. The advice given by the principal ideologues of shock therapy all came from the West. These relations tended to be asymmetric, whereas in terms of security arrangements Russia was largely treated as an equal at least from 1990 to 1992. The OSCE was the central security forum and NATO expansion may not have been on the table as much as it has been since the early 2000s.

In my reading, the processes and mechanisms of political economy were crucial in the causal complex shaping the transformation of Russia in the 1990s. In 1999, the Kosovo War (NATO started to bomb Yugoslavia in March 1999)[7] and the first NATO expansion in 1999 (the Visegrad countries joined in April 1999, except for Slovakia) contributed to the process by further alienating the Russian leadership from the West and from its interests and intentions. These developments started to shape modes of responsiveness and thereby interactions in the 2000s, the decade to which our discussion is about to turn next.

TF: Yes, let us move on to the 2000s. But, before that, I will just briefly comment on one point, namely whether I commit myself to some kind of essentialism when claiming that Russia's choices and its trajectory from the 1990s onwards were strongly shaped by internal factors. I do not think so, because putting emphasis on the internal factors does not deny the potential or limited role of external factors and interaction. There is no commitment to any suprahistorical essentialism if in some historical circumstances the primacy is placed on the internal factors. By contrast, if we deny the possibility that a state can be a certain kind of (aggressive) state mainly on the basis of its internal development, it would also represent some kind of (reverse) "essentialism". This is an empirical question and of course drawing a sharp line between internal and external is difficult.

In conclusion, we can tentatively state that several root causes of the war in Ukraine can be traced back to the 1990s. This is natural because – regressively – all causes of causes can be traced further back in history. It remains an open question as to what extent these developments might have been malleable in the sense that, in some instances, actors could have acted differently. In all probability there was no simple course that would lend itself to a "minimalistic rewriting" principle. Both the European security order and Russia's development in the 1990s were influenced by structural factors that could have been better, or could have opened up alternative futures only in some ideal cases. Nevertheless, these structures did not inevitably pave the way to the war in Ukraine in 2022.

Notes

1 In the 1990 OSCE document *Charter of Paris for a New Europe*, the participating states fully recognised "the freedom of States to choose their own security arrangements". In the 1999 OSCE *Istanbul Charter for European Security*, it was formulated as follows: "We reaffirm the inherent right of each and every participating State to be free to choose or change its security arrangements, including treaties of alliance, as they evolve. Each State also has the right to neutrality. Each participating State will respect the rights of all others in these regards".
2 In 1995–1996, I led a research project on EU–Russia relations at the Finnish Institute for International Affairs (see Patomäki 1996). In the late 1990s, I conducted several field trips to Russia with Christer Pursiainen as we studied the development of Russian civil society (see Patomäki & Pursiainen 1998; 1999; 2004).
3 Several objects of a physical nature have an essence that is independent of our concepts. As is presented by scientific realists, in these cases it is sensible

to talk about real categories that can be defined in relation to necessary features and forces. Water molecules consist of two hydrogen atoms and one oxygen atom that have been combined with a covalent bond. Water has emergent features. Under normal air pressure, water is a liquid that is between 0 and 100 degrees Celsius. Its greatest density is at 3.98 degrees Celsius and so on. There is no point in assessing these kinds of features and forces normatively. In contrast, social actions and structures are context-dependent, contingent, changeable and changing, and susceptible to several normative and other judgements. The critique of unchanging essence can be understood through the concept of contrast space. From an essentialist point of view, a contrast space is formed in terms of different actors with taken-for-granted characteristics (for example: a peaceful A, neutral B, and aggressive and oppressive C); whereas within a relational and processual understanding, the contrast space consists of a series of open-ended processes (A, B, C, etc.) whose effects include the creation of the identity, dispositions, and interests of the actors.

4 It is difficult for us to grasp our and others' existential and causal dependence on social wholes and processes because, as observers of socio-historical developments, we are enfolded within them. Some social theorists try therefore to alienate us from this familiarity, for example by developing "quantum social theories" (e.g. Wendt 2015). I agree, however, with Tony Lawson (2022) that there is no need to mystify processes that involve pre-existing relational and multicomponent objects (reflectively conscious and positioned social individuals), the powers of which are selectively exercised or enacted in interactions. These powers and the underlying structures are liable to change through interactions as well as experiences through various processes and their outcomes. These kinds of processual social theories have been systematically developed and discussed since the 1960s (e.g. Berger & Luckmann 1991/1966).

5 For example, Hans-Gert Pottering, an MEP from the EPP group, declared on 1 January 1994 that Russia can never become a member of the EU because it is too big and partly in Asia. However, in April 1994, Russia's Prime Minister Viktor Chernomyrdin stated that Russia was preparing a membership application. Agence Europe reported that EU actors were confused and failed to comment on the Russian intention. Russia was never formally prohibited from applying for EU membership but, since 1994, Russia has been de facto off the list of those countries that could, in principle, become members (for relevant documentation, see Patomäki 1996, 9–10).

6 The concept of *world time* refers to "the influence of changing forms of inter-societal system upon episodic transitions" (Giddens 1981, 24, borrows the concept from Eberhardt). An episodic transition that occurs in one historical conjuncture may have quite a different form, and quite different consequences, to an apparently similar episode in another conjuncture. Instead of talking about "inter-societal system" we could also analyse world time in terms of historically evolving fields of global political economy (as in Patomäki 2022a). For example, the re-emergence of global financial markets

in the 1960s and 1970s and the wave of financialisation that followed have enabled post-Soviet oligarchs to tap into global financial flows, invest in assets across the world typically through tax havens, and buy and sell property in search of fast profits in locations such as Geneva, London, or New York. The reamplification of the field of orthodox economic liberalism in the world economy has thus benefitted not only the post-Soviet oligarchs but also financial centres and tax havens, while hampering economic developments in Russia and Ukraine.

7 In the NATO bombings of Serbia and Kosovo, some 500 civilians died and 245,000 were forced to flee. The war was never declared and it did not have a UN mandate. The goal of the war was to change borders: to separate Kosovo from Yugoslavia. Putin's regime has referred to this episode repeatedly and sees (incorrectly) that it justifies similar action.

3 The 2000s
Wars, Revolutions, and Misfired Declarations

HP: Your conclusion about acting otherwise and the influence of history in the 1990s is somewhat different from my understanding. I see many plausible counterfactual possibilities: more realistic economic policies and favourable socio-economic developments in Russia and Ukraine; dissolving NATO at the end of the Cold War;[1] opening the possibility of EU membership to Russia; refraining from bombing Yugoslavia in the absence of UN authorisation, and so on. But let us move forward to the 2000s. It is not easy to cover the critical junctures and nodal points of this decade in a series of short comments, particularly because Russia's development is intertwined with much vaster global processes. Relevant processes tend to be overlapping and/or connected, while their causal effects can be delayed, self-reinforcing or mutually reinforcing, or, as is often the case, contradictory.

Putin rose to power in autumn 1999 and won the election the following summer. His project was to end the chaos in Russia. A key moment in the development of contemporary Russia was the agreement between Putin and the oligarchs. The wealth and socio-economic position of the oligarchs was secured in exchange for their support for Putin and state authority. Since the early 2000s, crime rates have decreased in Russia. For example, the number of murders is just a fraction of what it was at its worst. A limited sort of rule of law was duly established in Russia despite widespread corruption (Russia ranks alongside typical African and Latin American countries in corruption indices). During Putin's first two terms, economic growth was quite rapid and poverty was reduced. The state was again able to pay pensions and social benefits. The economic growth was facilitated by the rising price of oil and other raw materials in the world markets.

In autumn 1999, Putin had no political party to back him. The hastily assembled "Unity" grouping and its successor, the "United Russia" party, originally emphasised stability, which was to be achieved through pragmatic problem-solving. United Russia soon started to woo voters with conservative values and nationalism and, as time progressed, the party adopted more and more elements from the Eurasian ideology. The idea of a multipolar world and constructing a counterforce to US hegemony had already emerged in the 1990s, but was reinvigorated by the political changes and ideological shifts of the 2000s. United Russia is often associated with some sort of "central planning" interwoven with security services, including the police and army but, at the same time, many of its policies have been market-oriented. Putin has criticised neoliberalism on several occasions, but Russian tax policies, for example, are more neoliberal than in typical EU member states (Putin's government took up the neoliberal programme after Yeltsin in two areas, namely taxation and fiscal discipline; Rutland 2013, 340). In 2021, government expenditure in Russia amounted to about 36% of GDP, whereas in many EU countries it is close to 60% (in terms of share of value added or employment, the public sector is in all countries only a part of this; for example, in Finland this share is about 20–25%).

At the beginning of his term, Putin had discussions about Russia's possible NATO membership, but it soon became evident that Russia was not welcome in the military alliance, at least not on its own terms, including equality with the US (see e.g. Hoffman 2000; Rauch 2001). The 9/11 terrorist attacks and the subsequent wars in Afghanistan and Iraq happened during Putin's first term. There was a short moment after 9/11 when it seemed that the common threat of "Islamic terrorism" could bring Russia and the US closer together (at this stage Moscow approved, albeit reluctantly, the expansion of NATO). From a pragmatic perspective, perhaps Russia could achieve the position of a recognised superpower through cooperation with the US at a relatively low cost? The war in Iraq altered the situation, however (see e.g. Ambrosio 2005). Putin's Russia was strongly opposed to the war in Iraq and tried, together with France and China, to prevent it in the UN Security Council. The US and the UK decided to act without a UN mandate, which was interpreted by the Russian leadership as a blow against (1) international law and (2) Russia's position in international politics. Consequently, the emphasis on the importance of multipolarity reappeared in the speeches of Russian leaders and in Russian official statements, including those with other states.

In *The Political Economy of Global Security* (Patomäki 2008, 145–147), I argued that the administration of the younger Bush (first term 2001–2005) and especially the invasion of Iraq (2003) constituted a nodal point in world history. This nodal point involved a turn towards overt neo-imperialism, albeit in a context where the expansion of power is no longer dependent on the direct control of territory (cf. Hardt & Negri 2000). The basic concepts and ideas of this new imperialism were articulated, for example, in the US national security strategy, including:

(1) a universalist (and in effect also narcissistic) commitment to lead other nations towards "the single sustainable model for national success", that is, the American model of free markets and liberal democracy;
(2) readiness to use force unilaterally if needed, which amounts to a claim to the legitimate right of extra-territorial and in that sense imperial violence;
(3) a commitment to prevent the emergence of any military competitor to American global dominance, resembling the idea behind the two-power standard in naval armament that Britain adopted in 1889.

Although the US National Security Strategy of that era recognised the sovereignty of other "great powers" within their territory – and the need to have good relations with them – their right to extra-territorial violence was denied. The US was assumed to be exceptional. In the 2008 book, I hypothesised that the turn of the US towards neo-imperialism is likely to be a critical world-historical juncture because others will respond in kind, and thus it opens up a new era of competing imperialisms (partly analogous to the era of 1871–1914). The anticipated changes happened rapidly in Russia. First, there was a strong reaction against the invasion of Iraq. While the war continued, Putin's government succeeded, at least to some extent, in stabilising Russian society. Production was returning to levels of the Soviet era. The moment of worst "weakness" started to be over (the metaphor of weakness and strength constitutes many practices of international relations, including through great-power strategies). The colour revolutions of 2003–2005 occurred at this time as well. Both the Rose Revolution in Georgia and the Orange Revolution in Ukraine were responses to election fraud. In the case of Georgia, the opposition was trained and funded by the US. In the case of Ukraine, US and EU involvement may have been less clear (the extent of their involvement is a contested issue), but the opposition tried to expand the revolution to Russia and Belarus.

In the context of this nodal point, the Russian leadership tended to interpret the colour revolutions as strategic tools for the West's – involving the US, NATO, and the EU – eastward expansion (Patomäki 2018, ch. 3). The securitisation of these uprisings triggered exceptional countermeasures by the Russian side, which in turn have led to unintended counterproductive effects, not least in Georgia and Ukraine

(Delcour and Wolczuk 2015), to which Russia has again reacted (spiral of escalation; see also Michailova 2022). Also before the 2007–2008 elections, there was talk in Russia about the danger of a "colour revolution". Academic analysts have been torn between two different interpretations. Some argue that securitisation has served Putin's regime in domestic politics, whereas others think that the anxiety of leading Russian politicians is genuine (see Duncan 2013). The fear seems genuine, but do the dominant beliefs in Russia conflate concerns about the ruling elite's position and the interests of society at large? A plausible interpretation is that the domestic context exposed the Russian political system to securitisation, while securitisation on the other hand triggers measures that – especially if made permanent – tend to de-democratise society.

Through securitisation, the universalising programme of Western neoliberalism – manifest in various free-market arrangements, neighbourhood policies, and programmes of democracy and human rights promotion – came to be contested and geo-politicised. Russia turned to neo-revisionism criticising the one-sided nature of the rules of the international system without trying to change them (Sakwa 2016, 30–34). In its neo-revisionism, Russia has continued to combine elements of state capitalism and neoliberalism. A culmination point was reached at the 2008 Bucharest NATO summit, which started formal membership negotiations with Albania and Croatia and welcomed Ukraine and Georgia as future members. The Russian reaction was aggressive, announcing that Russia was considering the possibility of taking military and other steps along its borders if the two countries became part of the organisation (General Juri Balujevski quoted in *Deutsche Welle* 2008). The Russo-Georgian War started in August 2008, and it is widely held that one of Russia's aims was to prevent Georgia from joining NATO (e.g. Laaneots 2016, 11).

The 1990s formed the basis for the future by creating a context in which someone like Putin could rise to power. Still, at that stage, the confrontation between Russia and the West could have been avoided. To reiterate, the simultaneity of the Second Chechen War and the US war on terror created a situation where the pragmatic Putin regime saw an opportunity for Russia to promote its interests through cooperation in the context of the interconnected world economy on which Russia has been particularly dependent (although, during the Putin era, the ratio of exports to GDP has gradually declined from 70% to 46%). However, it is still unclear whether a mere common enemy could have formed a sufficient basis for long-term cooperation, given the substance of the

US Grand Strategy, on the one hand, and the ongoing repositioning of Russia, on the other, in terms of:

(1) Russia's increasing alienation from the "the single sustainable model for national success";
(2) the establishment of Russia as being permanently outside the EU and NATO;
(3) the principle of multipolarity that resurfaced after the wars in Kosovo and (especially) Iraq.

It is evident that the Iraq War was a turning point, as it demonstrated the incompatibility of the US and Russian positionings. Here, the US and the UK are responsible for the turning point: it would have been possible to act otherwise simply by complying with the will of the UN Security Council. In addition, when it comes to promoting civil society and supporting the colour revolutions, the problem lies in the idea that there is only one "single sustainable model" at the end of history (cf. Fukuyama's argument at the end of the Cold War). This has been a constitutive idea of the expansion of both the EU and NATO – while it has also been closely related to the acceptance of US hegemony (see Patomäki & Pursiainen 1998; Patomäki & Pursiainen 1999; Patomäki 2000).

The final mistake of the 2000s was to declare that NATO would expand to Georgia and Ukraine. This occurred concurrently with the deepening of the global financial crisis (GFC) in 2008–2009. The GFC constituted a new nodal point, paving the way for regressive developments involving the rise of nationalistic-authoritarian populism across the world. Nationalism and geopolitics were also becoming increasingly prevalent ideologically in Russia, as well as in relevant academic fields. As Andrei and Pavel Tsygankov (2021, 1) put it, "since the second half of the 2000s, Russian IR has been searching for nationally distinct values, perhaps as a protective response to political and cultural pressures by an alien Western civilization demanding compliance with its values and interests". In parallel with these developments and through various turns in Russian politics, the political system started to assume increasingly authoritarian characteristics.

TF: I agree with your analysis for the most part, but my emphasis is different. I see that the nodal point of the 2000s was between Putin's first and second terms, when Russia's foreign policy turned away from cooperation with the West towards Eurasianism and tighter cooperation with the so-called rising powers (BRICS). Putin's Berlin speech of 2001, which emphasised cooperation and European values, can be regarded as a signpost pointing in one direction, and the Munich speech of 2007, which challenged Western hegemony and actions, as a signpost pointing the opposite way.

This development, which led to the deterioration in relations between Russia and the West, had myriad causes and hence it is impossible to think that just one of them was decisive. However, if one event could be highlighted, the Ukrainian Orange Revolution of 2004 was, in my view, a clear turning point. The Kremlin interpreted it as a major Western challenge in its sphere of interest. What made it even worse was that it came as a personal blow to Putin. He visibly took part in Viktor Yanukovych's campaign, who was announced to have beaten his more Western-aligned competitor Viktor Yushchenko in the second round of the election. Yet the results were contested on the basis of the exit polls, and OSCE election observers reported fraud. The protests led to re-elections and, in the end, to Yushchenko's victory. We cannot go deeper into the details of this episode here, but the humiliation caused by the loss of one's own candidate and the fear of the spread of colour revolutions, combined with the interpretation that the West's insidious activities were behind everything (even though it was, at its core, just reactive support for democratic principles and in general much less invasive than Russia's actions), was a shock to Putin (Zygar 2016, 95). It was after this that friction with the West started to increase, leading to the famous speech at the Munich security conference in February 2007. As the Kremlin's frustration and bitterness grew, Russian foreign policy became more perseverant and ruthless. At the same time, the rapid economic growth that had continued since the early 2000s made a policy change challenging the West and the international order more feasible.

Of course, the Orange Revolution was not the only reason why the rapprochement with the West that Putin had started in his first term withered and turned into distrust and bitterness. The decision by Moldovan President Vladimir Voronin to reject the unilaterally drafted Russian plan to federalise the state to end the Transnistrian conflict, allegedly after EU High Representative Javier Solana had advised Voronin to do so, was a comparable experience (see Hill 2021). The Iraq War that the US started in breach of international law in 2003 likewise did nothing to contribute to better relations with the West. However, as you say, Russia was in the same boat as Germany and France, among others. But the hubris of the US affected Russia more deeply for two reasons. First, Russia's image of its relations with the US had still rested on the idea of parity. Second, the experience of betrayal was more personal as Putin remained in power. Russia's art of "whataboutism", responding to an accusation of wrongdoing by claiming that an offence committed by another is similar or worse, was strongly fuelled by that particular war, even though the West was not unanimous but divided. References to the West's double standards were understandable to a degree, but Russia's bitterness was also fed by its overall inability to see its own actions in the light of common standards, and to recognise, not to mention admit, its own mistakes. Such a pattern manifested itself several times in the 2000s, for example, when Russia was criticised by the West for the disproportionate use of violence in the Second Chechen War, or when responding to the terrorist attacks in Moscow in 2002 and in Beslan in 2004.

Applying the rule of minimalist rewriting, perhaps the most significant event that the West, and especially the US and NATO, could have easily avoided in the 2000s was, as you mention, the declaration at NATO's Bucharest 2008 summit according to which Georgia and Ukraine would become members of NATO.[2] This statement was both superfluous and contradictory because the more relevant decision at the summit was that these countries, due to the opposition from France and Germany, were not even taken into the Membership Action Plan (MAP), which would mark the first step towards their membership. For Russia, the demonstrative signal reflecting the ambition of the US was more galling, however. The direct causal relationship from the NATO summit declaration to the Georgia War is questionable, but it is easy to see that the declaration may have been a possible factor leading to the war.

After the shift in the Kremlin's perspective, the supposed mistreatment of Russia seemed to continue no matter how hard the West tried to normalise relations and take Russia into account, even by largely overlooking Russia's actions in Georgia. Neither the US "reset" policy nor the modernisation partnership with the EU were enough to change the course. In spite of expanding economic relations, and political cooperation across different areas, including some new initiatives, there was no breakthrough. Rather, the Kremlin concluded that the cooperative approach during Dmitri Medvedev's term was counterproductive. The new security agreement proposed by Russia was not endorsed by the West and hence it led nowhere, although it was by no means ignored to avoid disappointing Russia. The use of force against Muammar Gaddafi's Libya by a NATO-led coalition in 2011, which was possible because Russia abstained in the UN Security Council, was also seen as yet another sign of the West's tendency to exceed agreed boundaries, and duly provided one more reason for distrust towards the West.

When assessing the developments of the 2000s, we have to take Russia's domestic factors into consideration as well. Even though Putin was at least rhetorically supporting democracy, human rights, and the rule of law during the start of his term, at the core of his project was the construction of a strong state. Little by little, during the 2000s, the *siloviks*, representatives of "institutions of force", increased their power – and the term "securocracy" emerged in the early 2000s to describe Russia's political system (see e.g. Bremmer & Charap 2007). A central signpost for the concentration of power in the Kremlin was the trial and long prison sentence of the powerful oligarch and richest man in Russia, Mikhail Khodorkovsky, after he challenged Putin in October 2003. Simultaneously, the media was taken under tighter control and election manipulation increased. Russia was relegated from a "Partly Free" country to a "Not Free" country by Freedom House in 2005. The rise of the *siloviks* did not lead to any swift changes in Russia's overall foreign policy, but the style hardened and became visible, among other things, in the rising number of assassinations abroad: exiled Chechen leader Zelimkhan Yandarbiyev was murdered in Doha in 2004, and the defected agent Alexander Litvinenko in London in 2006. If we ask whether foreign relations explain domestic development or whether domestic developments explain foreign relations, or whether they run on their own tracks, we cannot provide a definitive answer. However, the story of the primacy of domestic factors is strong (see McFaul 2018; Belton 2020; Stoner 2021).

HP: We have at least one clear counterfactual in common, namely that the announcement at the 2008 NATO summit was an unnecessary provocation. Your interpretation of the 2003 Iraq War is akin to mine, but you are not explicit about whether the US and UK could and should have acted otherwise. We both see the colour revolutions of 2003–2005 as a tipping point in the development of the relationship between the West and Russia, but tend to interpret them somewhat differently. While you correctly deny the ahistorical essentialism concerning Russia's "character" and so forth, it seems to me that your analysis nonetheless involves a taken-for-granted contrast space that includes state actors with given characteristics (for example, democracy promoting A, neutral B, and aggressive C). Moreover, the US and the EU represent category A and Russia category C (cf. note 3 in Chapter 2). The same goes for your interpretation of "whataboutism". As you define it, "whataboutism" is clearly a fallacy because two wrongs do not make a right. On the other hand, attempts to rationalise or ignore the wrongdoings of the West do not help either because double standards are not only a moral issue but also have causal consequences. Double standards tend to undermine the credibility and legitimacy of the prevailing rules and principles. Moreover, actor formation is a process whereby internal and external developments are inseparable and interwoven. For example, securitisation means, among other things, de-democratisation inside a state.

One counterfactual concerns the positioning of Putin and his regime in relation to the oligarchs. For example, in the Khodorkovsky case you mentioned, the West supported a key oligarch, one of the richest men on earth and, at the same time, positioned itself against Putin in Russia's domestic affairs. I think this was probably a mistake. If Putin had taken the project of controlling the oligarchs further in accordance with the principles of the rule of law and democracy (bearing in mind, on the other hand, that Khodorkovsky accused Putin of corruption as well), then Russia could have developed in another direction even in the second half of the 2000s. I do not see any justification for the "oligarchs" and other super-rich controlling a significant part not only of Russia's but also of the world's wealth, and by doing so getting to greatly influence political and historical developments. The status and position of contemporary billionaires is a major pathology of the neoliberal era.

Notes

1 Each of these counterfactuals would require systematic analysis, which is unfortunately beyond the scope of our dialogue. For this reason, it is also not possible to delve into the "dissolution of NATO" counterfactual. The key question is: How different would the world have been if NATO had been dismantled in 1991–1992, and if the building of the post-Cold War "security architecture" had focused on developing common institutions in Europe and globally? It can be argued – as I tend to believe – that the subsequent developments would have been more cooperative, although causal complexes always include multiple components and open systems are shaped by extrinsic forces (cf. my critical analysis of the rationale for the continued existence of NATO after the end of the Cold War in Patomäki 2003). One of the anonymous referees of our manuscript raised the question that if in fact the continued existence of NATO and its "expansion was a crucial underlying explanatory factor, why did NATO expand in this way?". The relevant causal complex has evolved temporally, at different moments manifold inter- and intrarelated components, including multiple actors from those forming the US military-industrial complex to Eastern European political parties and states, not to speak of the organisation of NATO itself. However, as far as the choice between OSCE, on the one hand, and NATO, on the other is concerned, the leadership or hegemony of the US seems to have played a major role. As TF has written, "The leadership position of the United States goes a long way in explaining why NATO survived and became stronger and why, for example, the OSCE did not develop into Europe's central security organization" (Forsberg 2002, 43). Alan Cafruny et al. (2022, 2) put it more bluntly in the current context: "[A] central underlying factor in the conflict

is the Anglo-American desire to consolidate NATO as a vehicle for political and military domination in Europe".
2 Other issues where the West could have been more forthcoming included the Treaty on the Conventional Armed Forces in Europe, and missile defence in eastern Europe.

4 The 2010s
The War in Ukraine Starts

TF: Although we have already touched upon the beginning of the 2010s, the actual turning point of the decade was the Ukraine crisis in 2013, the annexation of Crimea and the war in eastern Ukraine that followed in 2014. Were these events necessary causes of the 2022 war in Ukraine that Russia started? Moreover, could the crisis, the annexation, and the war have been avoided in some sustainable way if the development up to 2013 is taken as given? I think that the answer to both questions is "maybe", but to the latter one the "maybe" is perhaps so qualified that it is almost a "no".

Let us start with domestic developments. The re-election of Putin in 2012 solidified the power of the clique that had been formed around the security services. Putinism started to be even more authoritarian, and it can be said that Putin became a prisoner of his own creation. He could no longer stand back. There were several anti-government protests in Russia in 2011–2013 in support of free elections, democracy, and civil rights, which did not lead to desirable outcomes and were suppressed with the use of force and by restricting civil rights. Putin's return to the presidency was also accompanied by a discursive change, which made spheres of influence thinking, the use of military force, and the Crimean annexation normal (see Hopf 2016).

As such, the Maidan protest movement in Ukraine, which erupted after President Viktor Yanukovych refused to sign an association agreement with the EU, but then switched its focus to the corruption and abuse by the government, and resulted in the suspension of Yanukovych and his subsequent exile, took the Kremlin by surprise. The West, and especially the EU, were driven into this crisis unintentionally and unprepared. By supporting the Euromaidan protest movement in Ukraine, both the US and the EU, from the perspective of the Kremlin, were once again stepping on its toes. Russia had no wish to allow Ukraine to conclude a bilateral treaty with the EU without trilateral arrangements. When Russia was not able to control the events in Ukraine, it acted reactively as well as opportunistically, carrying out threats that it had warned about previously. Both the annexation of Crimea and most probably also the support for east Ukrainian separatism were both planned in advance. However, Russia did not have any clear idea about the international repercussions of the annexation of Crimea, and even less about how to resolve the Ukraine question in a sustainable manner. Despite various documented studies about the 2014 Ukrainian crisis, many details are still unclear and contested. The exact role of the West in the crisis is one of them, to the extent that it had not just supported but also "orchestrated" the whole coup. The West had its hopes and preferences, but the outspoken aim of the Western mediators in the Ukraine crisis in 2014 was to stop the violence and let the Ukrainians decide about their future through a democratic process. Those who believe that the West was able to dictate the outcome have to see its action as amazingly successful, given that Russian attempts to intervene in Ukrainian domestic politics were much more massive and long-standing. Indeed, what is clear is Russia's blatant violation of international law, which undermined the fundaments of the European security order. The sin of the West was omission, while Russia's sin was commission.

Counterfactually thinking, we can ponder what would have happened if the EU had not offered the association agreement to Ukraine. On the one hand, it is possible that some kind of crisis might have erupted at some point in Ukraine in any case. As people were dissatisfied with the regime and corruption was rampant, the presidential election scheduled for 2015 had been contentious. On the other hand, if the Euromaidan protests in Ukraine had not mushroomed, the EU would most likely have simply accepted the outcome that concluding the association agreement with Ukraine had failed. There were no last-minute attempts to persuade Yanukovich to sign the treaty, but only the hope that Ukraine might do so in the future. When Armenia decided against signing its association agreement with the EU, representatives on the EU side protested against Moscow's influence on Yerevan's decision, but the EU did nothing to reverse it.

Or let us imagine what would have happened if the West had not supported the Euromaidan protests in 2014. This question often assumes that if the West had not supported the protest movement, it would not have been able to oust Yanukovych. This assumption in itself is questionable, but let us assume so for the sake of the counterfactual. In that case, Ukraine would have slid into Russia's sphere of influence just as Belarus has. The idea of a neutral and "Finlandised" Ukraine flourishing between the EU and Russia would have been a "realist delusion" (cf. Mearsheimer 2015, 2018, who talks about liberalism as "the great delusion") since the Kremlin did not respect a separate Ukrainian identity.[1] In order to remain at least a partial democracy and an economically successful area, the fragmented and corrupted country would have needed a strong uniting leader, who would not have resorted to the Lukashenko type of oppression and dictatorship. A successful emulation of Finland's "Finlandisation" during the Cold War was unlikely in the case of Ukraine, as Finland's success was anchored in such factors that were lacking in Ukraine before 2014, such as national unity and robust state institutions (Forsberg & Pesu 2016). It must be noted that the crisis in Ukraine in 2013 did not start because Ukraine aspired to join NATO, but because of a cooperation agreement with the EU. Ukraine's slide towards Russia would have probably led to strong repression and at least to the rise of violence domestically. In addition to this, there are no guarantees that Russia's control of Ukraine would have contained its neo-imperialist ambitions and possible further aggression, even though Ukraine and Belarus have held a special position in Russia's identity-based geopolitics. After achieving a tight east Slavic trinity, the Kremlin could have set its sights on Moldova and Kazakhstan, for example, which have Russian-speaking minorities (see Coalson 2014).

After 2014, Russia's relationships with both Ukraine and the West decayed even more. The sanctions against Russia, and Russia's countersanctions in response, did not prevent economic interaction and diplomatic communication, but a strategic partnership entailing close cooperation on security issues was out of the question. The suggestions of a new "grand bargain" between Russia and the West were dead on arrival because the principles were too ambivalent, and there was no sense of urgency and no mutual trust between parties. However, it was already obvious after 2014 that the risk of a military escalation that might lead to a full-scale war between Russia and Ukraine, or even Russia and the West, could not be ruled out (see Forsberg & Haukkala 2016, 247). An escalation of the military conflict was, however, not seen as likely because it was assumed that Putin knew the risks and avoided taking big risks: in other words, acting ruthlessly but only step by step and not taking a gamble with it. As the West did not want to corner Russia, the sanctions were more symbolic in nature, which duly enabled the continuation and even further solidification of Putin's regime, while also creating a new normal in the West–Russia relationship (whereby Trump's term was riddled with question marks). The West could not discard the normative principles regarding Russia's violations of international law and thus had no option of lifting the sanctions without

Russia acting first. The West's strategy was to wait and see: neither to yield nor to provoke, in the hope that some opportunities might arise with a possible change in the Russian leadership so that a constructive relationship based on mutual understanding would become possible again. Russia may have cherished similar hopes with regard to the leadership changes in the West, but the Kremlin may have been disappointed with Trump and did not see any prospect with Biden, although the latter wanted to establish "a stable, predictable relationship". This imaginary new normal did not satisfy Russia, and the downward spiral in the relationship between Russia and the West continued. This was visible in Aleksey Navalny's poisoning and imprisonment, in the manipulation of the refugee crisis at Europe's borders, as well as in the increased information operations in the West and across the globe.

Many politicians in the West believe that harder and more determined actions against Russia in the earlier crises would have prevented the 2022 war in Ukraine (see e.g. Agrawal 2022). Was the Kremlin let off the hook too easily with the war in Georgia (in 2008), as well as with the Crimean annexation and the subsequent war in east Ukraine, leading it to imagine that the West would not react much more strongly in 2022? I do not think that we can give any definitive answer, since we lack evidence. The failure of deterrence in 2022 does not necessarily mean that the West could have deterred Russia successfully with the available means in the earlier crises even if they had been employed. They could have caused the escalation of the conflict already earlier. Nevertheless, this is surely one counterfactual we should ponder.

HP: It is obvious that, taken together, the Ukrainian crisis of 2013, the subsequent occupation of Crimea, and the war in eastern Ukraine in 2014 constituted a key nodal point of the 2010s, but to understand events and processes, we have to take a few steps back in time. The global financial crisis (GFC) began in 2007 and critically shaped the development of the world economy during 2008–2009, while also altering political tendencies (prior neoliberalisation had created the context for the rise of nationalistic-authoritarian populism through various constitutive effects, increasing inequalities and vulnerability to crises, and generating existential insecurity; Patomäki 2021). The GFC triggered the euro crisis, which then continued for years (2010–2015). These crises affected Ukraine as well (for a more detailed political economy analysis, see Patomäki 2018, ch. 3).

The socio-economic development of Ukraine at the end of the 1990s and early 2000s was similar to that of Russia and largely caused by the same factors. The liberal and chaotic 1990s were followed by rapid economic growth between 2000 and 2008, which lifted people out of poverty and improved general socio-economic conditions. Prior to the Euromaidan revolution and its aftermath was the social conflict that boiled over between the years 2008 and 2009, and the massive 15% GDP drop that Ukraine experienced as a consequence of the GFC. The economic collapse led to rising inequality and uncertainty, and fostered antagonistic attitudes. Ukraine was soon battling the conditionalities of the IMF and the EU neighbourhood programme. After a brief partial recovery, the economic recession continued alongside the euro crisis and was partly caused by it. Ukraine drifted into deep indebtedness and its external reserves dwindled rapidly.

Demonstrations were organised immediately after the Ukrainian government stopped preparing for the EU's association agreement in November 2013. The acute phase of the economic crisis in Ukraine was concurrent with the Euromaidan demonstrations, which was no coincidence. The EU had offered a relatively small loan with similar conditions offered by the troika of international institutions for the crisis-ridden euro countries (the case of the collapse of the Greek economy shows where austerity can lead). Debates about these conditions were enmeshed with various social divisions in Ukraine, often reinforcing them by resonating with regional, linguistic, and political differences, which in turn were entangled with different interpretations of history. The social and political divides were also deepened by active attempts by the US, the EU, and Russia to influence Ukraine's development.

The EU's neighbourhood programme and association agreement are not neutral or "innocent" initiatives, but tend to have effects of power. These programmes and related agreements consist of an archetypal combination of neoliberal economic policy and a narrow liberalist view of human rights and democracy. Regarding external relations, the EU's relationship with Russia had already been permanently defined as an *external* relationship since the 1990s. In addition, the EU's internal documents acknowledge that "the idea that Europe is an exclusively 'civilian power' does not do justice to an evolving reality" (EU 2016, 2). Actors representing the EU may continue to associate the Union with a post-Westphalian, nonterritorial, 21st-century globalising system, but the effects of their own acts of border-drawing and securitisation are not under their control; meanings and dispositions have real constitutive and causal effects, many of which are unintended.

Russia's current leadership may rely on 19th-century vocabulary more clearly than the leaders of the EU and the US but, as Mearsheimer (2015) – whom you cite – has stated, the American (and in general, Western) quest to spread democracy, human rights, and free markets tends to involve attempts to bring pro-Western and pro-American governments to power, which implies the promotion of certain geopolitical interests and visions, whether acknowledged as such or not.[2] The attempt to separate Ukraine from Russia's "orbit" and bring it closer (a spatial metaphor prone to territorial interpretations) to the West has been part of this quest.

Accusations revolving around the outdated and problematic concept of "sphere of influence" have been common, and have not only been levelled in one direction. Here my point requires a little bit of historical background. As far as I know, the history of the concept is relatively short. It is often said to originate from the Monroe Doctrine (1823), but in my opinion one can only infer the concept from President James Monroe's 1823 speech as he did not use the term as such ("sphere of influence" or "sphere of interest").[3] The term and concept became common and gained a recognised position in international law during the neo-imperial period of 1871–1914, especially from the 1880s onwards. After World War II, which discredited the concept, there was a tacit and reciprocal understanding between the US and the USSR about "spheres of interest" but, although they recognised these spheres in practice, neither side used the term, and they would not have publicly approved of its use about their own country. Paul Keal (1983, 155) explains that the US was publicly committed to the sovereign equality of states and the norms of interstate behaviour, whereas the USSR framed its actions in terms of socialist solidarity. Then came the end of the Cold War. In the subsequent euphoria, it was widely thought that "sphere of interest" was an outdated concept that the world had finally shed – although, as far as I can see, the US has held on to its version of the tacit concept all along, and in a sense even globalised it. Since the mid-2000s, Russia has returned to geopolitical doctrines that, at least to an extent, resemble some of the ways in which the concept was used from the 1880s until 1945.

This is the broader context in which recent debates about "geopolitics" have been set. The more specific context involves a new phase in securitisation that was reached in Russia in 2013–2014. Since Ukraine's Euromaidan, the Russian leadership has framed mass anti-regime protests at home and abroad as a military threat (Bouchet 2016). The reactionary viewpoint of the Russian leadership has evolved accordingly: the fact that Crimea could be part of Ukraine, and Ukraine part of NATO, implies the possibility of American military bases in Crimea (the US has at least 600 military bases outside of its borders). As is evident, for instance, based on struggles over possible locations of US military bases in Central Asia,[4] these kinds of bases have been consistently perceived as a threat to Russia's "legitimate security interests".

I think geopolitical framings and such lines of reasoning can and should be criticised, but double standards should not be accepted in this case either. The US has followed the Monroe Doctrine since the 19th century and was ready to risk nuclear war because of similar regional security interests in 1962.[5] During the later phases of the Cold War, the US defended its "legitimate interests" in Central America, often by means of violence and war. If anything, the US Grand Strategy that was adopted in the early 2000s can be see as a (at least partial) globalisation of the tacit concept, to increasingly cover all of the hemispheres of the globe.

The overall context involves manifold contradictions. In particular, the universalising principles of human rights, the rule of law, and democracy are not compatible with absolutist interpretations of state sovereignty, which is nonetheless at the heart of the idea that states have an unqualified "freedom to join any alliance" regardless of the consequences (for a moderate immanent critique in terms of J.S. Mill's no-harm principle and OSCE agreements, see Patomäki 2022b). Moreover, neutrality – and especially military non-alignment – is compatible with a variety of different social orders and does not necessarily imply "a strong uniting leader like Kekkonen", not to mention Lukashenko. During the Cold War, Finland and Sweden were in fact exceptionally democratic, with a pluralist party system and a very active citizenry and civil society. What makes the situation difficult is that both sides want Ukraine to "gravitate towards their orbits". This can have consequences in a country as corrupt and divided as Ukraine (which now seems united as it defends itself against the aggressor, but has gone through phases of antagonism and even violent conflict during past decades). Still, neutrality and non-alliance are things that can be institutionally guaranteed internally (e.g. with a constitution) and externally (with agreements). For me, the assumption that Russia's dominance can only be avoided by being a member of NATO and/or the EU is groundless and implies a zero-sum game liable to instigate further escalation of the conflict. Linguistic expressions have performative effects.

You point out that proposals for a new security arrangement "were dead on arrival because the principles were too ambivalent, and there was no sense of urgency and no mutual trust between parties", but there were two reasons for this: (1) the hard will[6] of the West to further its ideas and interests as the universal truth that cannot be questioned or altered, and (2) Russia's hard will to oppose this world system in terms of such an understanding of pluralism that would, for its part, take the world further towards a 19th-century-style system of competing empires.[7] This is not very far from what you yourself have written, indicating that the EU–Russia conflict is a tragedy, where neither side wants the outcome, "but at the same time both have been unable to alter the policies that have contributed to the problem in the first place" (Forsberg & Haukkala 2016, 1, also 226). The erosion of trust has been mutual. The likely assassinations ordered by Putin's government and its active propaganda have played their part in this erosion, but even at the risk of accusations of "whataboutism", it is worthwhile remembering that these kinds of activities are not unique to Russia.[8] Escalation of a conflict is a process whereby both sides accuse each other of various outcomes of the escalation process or things associated with it. The annexation of Crimea violated international law and escalated the conflict to the brink of a great war, but it was only one step in a process that was a long time coming – and Russia tried to justify it by referring to the one-sided Kosovo independence declaration of 2008.

Despite all these critical comments and remarks, my conclusion may not look radically different from yours. Was there a possibility to act otherwise in the early 2010s? (I primarily think of the EU and the West more generally, but the choices made by Ukraine were also relevant here.) For me, the answer is yes, but a reserved yes, in the sense that both parties had established a *will* that is difficult to change (see note 6). The case of Greece in 2015 indicates how difficult it is to change the EU even from the inside. Furthermore, as you state, securitisation, ideological changes, and the dynamics of power on the Russian side have driven it increasingly towards authoritarianism, which has contributed to deepening the conflict with the West, which promotes "democracy, human rights, and free markets". In Russia, Western aspirations have often been taken to imply the ousting of Putin. For many Russians, Putin symbolises the return of order, some welfare, and possibly the resurrection of Russia's position in world politics. What is more, there are suspicions that the West tries to weaken Russian accords with the American Grand Strategy of preventing the emergence of competitors. Leaving aside the US and NATO, and focusing on the EU, acting otherwise would have required a major coalition for changing the fundamental rules and principles of the EU, as its external relations reflect its internal constitutive principles (which have been, in part, originally established elsewhere in international law, for example in GATT/WTO and the UN).

To put it differently, if we follow the rule of "minimal rewriting", then the relevant counterfactuals about 2013–2014 concern particular actions and decisions taken by actors within a given framework. The most immediate conflict in 2013–2014 was not about NATO membership but EU programmes. If fundamental changes had occurred before Euromaidan, they should have emerged from Russia's domestic struggles, the global financial crisis in 2008–2009, or the euro crisis in

2010–2015. As you mentioned, Russia's opposition was suppressed with violence and legal and other restrictions. Putin has continued to be approved by the politically indifferent and passive Russian population.

As far as the West is concerned, there have been forces of change inside the EU, but they came nowhere near to changing the EU during the 2000s and early 2010s.[9] NATO's pursuit of expansion continued during this era. There was no significant US opposition to prevailing economic and foreign policies before the rise of Bernie Sanders and Donald Trump in the 2016 presidential election (see Monthly Review 2022 for Sanders' analysis of the double standards of US foreign policy and the war in Ukraine). It seems probable that, for Russia, Yanukovych served as insurance against Ukrainian NATO membership. An analysis of Ukraine's domestic counterfactuals would take us into the murky waters of interpreting what really happened in Ukraine during those months, although it seems fair to argue that attempts to homogenise language in the linguistically and culturally diverse Ukraine have been part of the problem (many in Ukraine have shared a nationalist-populist understanding of language with their counterparts in other countries). It might be time to move on to the next stage, however, which – for me – starts in 2015.

TF: Agreed. I would just like to comment on a couple of things at this point though. To what extent is it relevant to refer to the violations of international law or other wrongdoings by the US or other Western actors? To what extent do these actions help us explain Russia's decision to start a full-scale war in Ukraine in 2022? At worst, such suggestions represent a type of "whataboutism", the main function of which is to draw attention away from Russia's actions. If the goal is to explain Russia's actions, questions about the normative condemnation of the West will sidetrack us. Equally problematic is if references to the US are being held as evidence of what is "normal" in international politics and, in that sense, rational. Russia is almost always compared only to the US and, even then, the policies of the US and Russia – typically norm violations – are rarely parallel. For example, while the Iraq War was based on false pretences of an alleged nuclear weapon programme, the long-lasting violence and blatant human rights violations against neighbouring countries and the domestic population were undisputed. The status of Kosovo was negotiated within a multilateral framework and a majority of states have recognised its independence. By the same token, the request to extradite hacker and whistleblower Julian Assange, no matter how disproportionate it might be, is not comparable with the attempt to assassinate a domestic opposition politician with chemical weapons. Most countries do not commit such crimes, so we have to ask why Russia does this. If Russia acts like this with regard to its domestic opposition, it makes the decision to wage war on other sovereign states more understandable.

References to wrongdoings and norm violations committed by the US and the West can help us understand Russia's politics and decisions if they have had a causal impact on Russia's foreign policy thinking. As I noted before, the Iraq War or the Libyan interventions, for example, may have contributed to Russia's frustration and suspicion towards the West. Yet instead of trying to strengthen the international norms together with Germany, for example, Russia decided to break them even more recklessly.

By the same token, there have been some attempts to defend the idea of "spheres of influence" as a functioning security arrangement. As practical arrangements coupled with the principle of prudence between the great powers, they may sometimes stabilise the international order. Yet it is very hard to justify such arrangements normatively. Advocates who criticise the wholesale rejection of the concept admit that "spheres of influence should not be viewed as normative propositions justifying a great power's right to dominate a region" (O'Rourke & Shifrinson 2022, 107). References to US policies and its Monroe Doctrine are not very persuasive arguments in relation to Russia and Ukraine, because we should reject sphere of influence practices of any state.

HP: If you allow me, I would like to respond briefly before we continue to the analysis of the final steps leading to the 2022 war (I will ignore your comment on Assange due to lack of space and mention only that there were discussions in the CIA about his assassination[10] and that Assange's persecution has lasted for over a decade and destroyed his health). I see your critique of "whataboutism" partly as an ontological question. You emphasise the separateness of Russian society and developments, and the intrinsic nature of Russia's actions. This presupposes some sort of atomism or individualism as applied to international society.[11] Such individualism has far-reaching consequences in terms of both ethics and social scientific explanations.[12] It can also be read as an argument along the lines of "it does not matter what the US and the EU do or what happens in the world economy, Russia is Russia, and it alone is responsible for its being and actions". It goes without saying that to demand moral or legal responsibility is not wrong per se. We can analyse the responsibility of actors in different situations, although it requires answers to questions concerning (1) the relationship between individual and collective responsibility, (2) what the applicable moral and legal rules may be, and so on. Moreover, as you also indicate, reasons for action are part of causal complexes. Therefore, it is in part also an empirical question as to whether US and, more broadly, Western actions, as perceived and interpreted in Russia, were involved in Russia's decision to start a full-scale war in Ukraine in 2022. In other words, whether the war can be explained in terms of the intrinsic nature of Russia *or* in terms of interactions in the wider context of international relations, world economy, and world time?

More generally, and independently of the possibility of attributing moral and legal responsibility for actions, the world is neither atomistic nor individualistic. In interstate relations, words and actions have both performative and causal effects, and these effects tend to be part of those geohistorical processes through which actors and structures are (re)produced and transformed. While I agree entirely that we should deny "sphere of influence" thinking in all cases (the US, Russia, and others), the existence of such spheres in the case of a leading state has performative and causal consequences. Similarly, the world economy is an interconnected system in which all countries are entangled – even the Soviet Union was in many ways part of the world economy[13] – and within which collective actors such as states are being formed and positioned. Worldwide division of labour, uneven but interconnected processes of growth, and dynamic relations of (inter)dependence shape developments in every corner of the globe (Patomäki 2022a).

Regarding "whataboutism", the apparent fact that the US is inclined to position itself above international law violates the principle of the rule of law. As the US has been perceived as hegemonic, the constitutive and causal effects of its words and deeds are more significant than those of most other states. Causation must also be understood processually. The legitimacy of law erodes if it is apparent that a leading state is assumed to be above or outside the rule of law. According to the principle of generalisability, a systematically inconsistent application cannot be sustainable (for example the authority of the International Criminal Court has deteriorated because of its highly selective processes; see Piccolo-Koskimies 2021). When there is no universal and legitimate principle of the rule of law, a highly selective application of law tends to mean the acceptance and legitimation of unilateral use of power. A unilateral denial by others of this kind of selectivity is, in turn, a step towards a kind of "anarchy", where the interpretation of the law is left to actors themselves, in the case of international law to sovereign states (while this has been the problem of international law all along, cf. Koskenniemi 2005).

Legitimacy can also be assessed normatively. The idea that a particular actor is above the law, but demands that everyone else abides by it, is in essence an argument for a "universal monarchy" (to use the

European term that originates from the Middle Ages and later found its way into Immanuel Kant's writings, for example) or "universal dictatorship" (as an analogy for Carl Schmitt's justification of dictatorship). A king – or, in today's world, a "leader" – is above the law but demands that their subjects follow the law and obey orders. The French Revolution was to a large extent about challenging the exceptionality of the sovereign king. The famous "dialectic of master and slave" by G.H.F. Hegel made the French Revolution and the overall struggle for the equality of subjects the universal principle of world history (I have analysed Hegel's thinking from a cosmopolitan perspective: Patomäki 1995). The principle of balance of power was originally meant to preserve pluralism in the European state system, but it could neither sustain peace nor establish the rule of law in international relations. Alexander Wendt (2003) has used the Hegelian logic of reciprocal recognition of the equality of humans as citizens in his argument on the "inevitability of a democratic world state". My view has long been that processes can go in the other direction as well: the world can descend towards a Hobbesian "anarchy" (cf. Wendt 1999, 270). When the world descends deeper in this direction, also through the effects of political economy mechanisms, the possibility of a great war is acute (on the interaction of fields, see Patomäki 2022a, chs 6–8). The world we see right now in front of us is a result of this kind of regression.

Notes

1 John Mearsheimer's (2015) interpretation of the crisis in Ukraine, its causes, consequences, and solutions has gained much attention as he has blamed the West for the crisis. His analysis is substantially messy and theoretically contradictory, however. Mearsheimer's theory of offensive realism starts from the assumptions that great powers want to widen their spheres of influence and weaken their competitors. If great powers act like this, then why should the West have given up Ukraine to Russia's sphere of influence? Besides, according to his theory, Russia's desire to expand to Ukraine should not depend on the actions of the West because great powers try to expand anyway: you cannot trust anyone. Furthermore, according to Mearsheimer (2015, 9), Putin was a master strategist and Ukraine's occupation would be akin to "swallowing a porcupine". If this is the case, Putin should not have attacked Ukraine, and the West would not have believed that he would. His writings since the war started have become even more incomprehensible. Suffice it to provide just one example of his argumentative style and content: "As it turns out, I have written a book about lying in international politics … and it is clear to me that Putin was not lying" (Mearsheimer 2022).

I already mentioned that Mearsheimer (1993) had also opined that Ukraine should not have given up its nuclear weapons.

2 I agree (with TF in note 1) that Mearsheimer's (2015) analysis is theoretically contradictory. He gives agency only to the West, while Russia merely realises the necessary law-like regularities of great-power politics. There are no such regularities in world politics or anywhere else in society or in any open system. However, this does not mean that Mearsheimer's analysis contains no insights, which he moreover may share with scholars from different theoretical backgrounds. For example, Mearsheimer's observation that it is not what the leaders of the Western countries themselves say NATO's intentions are, but how they are perceived in Russia, is important. Any student of misperceptions or social construction in international politics could argue that. Moreover, critical theorists and Marxists can easily share Mearsheimer's idea that the US and Western promotion of democracy, human rights, and free markets has tended to be enmeshed with interests and visions that either stem from profit making (which has oftentimes been articulated in terms of free trade, but property relations or access to raw materials or markets can be securitised and interdependence weaponised), or from security concerns articulated in terms of geopolitics by specialised actors occupying particular positions in the state apparatus, especially military planners.

3 Monroe merely referred to "this hemisphere", meaning the continent of the Americas. It seems that Monroe's expression was later generalised to include different "spheres" and different actors. President James Monroe's seventh annual message to Congress on 2 December 1823 is available here, for example: www.archives.gov/milestone-documents/monroe-doctrine.

4 Possible locations that have been under US consideration include Tajikistan, Kyrgyzstan (where the US had a base until 2014 despite "two revolutions and repeated attempts by Moscow to get it closed"), and Uzbekistan, which in the early 2020s seems the most likely candidate. However, "the issue of hosting U.S. troops in Uzbekistan will inevitably be met with resistance from Moscow and Beijing, and it's doubtful that Tashkent is prepared to pay that price. Moscow is already vocal in its criticism of many of Tashkent's initiatives, believing that Washington is behind them and that their ultimate aim is to weaken Central Asia's links with Russia" (Umarov 2021).

5 It is good to remember that the Ukrainian border is as close to Moscow as Cleveland in Ohio or Charlotte in North Carolina is to Washington DC (Havana in Cuba is three times farther).

6 "[T]he closure of the decision-making system from all extra messages that might influence the decision, is the key to the formation of the will" (Deutsch 1963, 111).

7 Cafruny et al. (2022) phrase a parallel idea in terms of a collision between the grand strategies of the US and Russia, going as far as to argue that "The collision of these grand strategies has triggered simultaneously a struggle for Ukrainian sovereignty and independence and a U.S.-Russia proxy war".

8 During the Cold War, the US made more than 50 violent interventions and bombed 25–30 different countries in various conflicts and wars. The list includes involvement in 35 assassination attempts that targeted foreign leaders or important politicians (Blum 2002, 125–167; more analytically, Galtung 2002, 94). The end of the Cold War has not decreased but rather increased the US tendency to get involved in developments of foreign states. Noteworthy is also the treatment of Julian Assange in the West (including in Sweden), which is not that far from the fate of Navalny in Russia. As the EU has largely been a civil power, it has tried to influence other states through loans and conditionalities, economic sanctions, and propaganda. These methods are of course more civilised than direct violence or enforcement.

9 I am leaving aside the proposed European Constitution that was rejected in 2005 in referendums held in France and the Netherlands, and which would not have changed that much. One of the weak forces for change has been the EuroMemo Group. Since 1997, the group has produced a critical memorandum each year about the EU's economic and political situation, and presented alternatives. The memo is signed each year by hundreds of experts on economics and political economy. The group has been affiliated with European left-wing social democracy, in the broad meaning of the term, and has tried to influence decision-making. The memos have addressed various crises and problematic developments, including the euro crisis and the rise of nationalist populism. Even though a few ideas on European financial policy and ecosocial transformation have been implemented in some restricted sense since the beginning of the 2020s, EuroMemo has not had much influence. See www.euromemo.eu/ (HP is the vice chair of the group in 2021–2022).

10 Wikipedia 2022 explains: "According to former intelligence officials, in the wake of the Vault 7 leaks, the CIA plotted to kidnap Assange from Ecuador's London embassy, and some senior officials discussed his potential assassination. Yahoo! News found 'no indication that the most extreme measures targeting Assange were ever approved.' Some of its sources stated that they had alerted House and Senate intelligence committees to the plans that Pompeo was suggesting. In October 2021, Assange's lawyers introduced the alleged plot during a hearing of the High Court of Justice in London as it considered the U.S. appeal of a lower court's ruling that Assange could not be extradited to face charges in the U.S.".

11 Methodological individualism in its original form (Schumpeter – Weber) merely meant that social explanations must refer to individual actors and their intentional actions. Later in the 20th century, individualism was associated with rational choice theory, the assumptions of which come close to the 17th-century Hobbesian atomism according to which individual and collective actors are formed spontaneously due to intrinsic causes, like mushrooms after rain. The nature of actors (in terms of their psychology, utility functions, etc.) can be deduced abstractly without any references to social contexts, interactions, processes, or mechanisms. "Some

mushrooms are just poisonous". In IR theory, Waltzian neorealism is sometimes associated with individualism in this sense, while Wendtian social constructivism is habitually seen as its antipode. The difference between the two can perhaps be seen even more clearly in state-based area studies (individualism) and approaches such as peace research and global political economy that emphasise the interconnected nature of the world (holism). The former comes close to methodological nationalism, the latter to methodological globalism (for a critique of methodological nationalism in contemporary IPE, see Kotilainen & Patomäki 2022, 95–96).

12 A variety of thinkers from Jean Piaget, J.M. Keynes, Hans Morgenthau, and Johan Galtung to Jacques Derrida have situated the foundations of morality in the ability to see things from the perspective of others and/or in the understanding that the actions of the Other are always to some extent caused or produced by the self (what you yourself do has effects on how "good" and "bad" possibilities in the Other come into being). This is also the methodological basis of double-hermeneutic and critical social sciences and constructivist IR theory.

13 This has been a point of contestation among political economists and social scientists. On the one hand, it is plausible to argue that the USSR was always tied to the developments in the capitalist world economy. For example, the USSR adopted Taylorism developed by Western capitalist firms early on, while systematic techniques of planning were developed simultaneously by market corporations in the West. The USSR imported technology and industrial goods and exported primary products and fossil fuels (I am simplifying and leaving aside developments over time). The USSR used world market prices in economic planning and hard currency for trade with the Western industrialised countries, except Finland, and most Third World countries. On the other hand, one can also argue that the share of foreign trade was relatively low (e.g. 4% of GDP), that world markets played only an indirect role in state planning, and that private property rights for the means of production did not exist. For an insightful Cold War-era review of this lively and complicated debate, see Gorin (1985).

5   2021–2022

Coercive Diplomacy and the Outbreak of War

HP: It may well be that we cannot agree on the issue of double standards or "whataboutism", so let us move on to the start of the war itself. As we know, after Crimea and Donbas, there were negotiations. The Minsk agreement was concluded in 2014 and renegotiated in 2015, but the implementation of Minsk II was postponed for years. In December 2016, I wrote in my blog that:

> The risk of escalation of the war in Ukraine is significantly larger than zero. Escalation is possible also against the wishes of Russia's leadership or any other party. The risk is so great and consequences so unpredictable that the conflict should not be left to evolve on its own, not to talk of its deliberate escalation. Even though the fear of a full-scale war can make the participants more cautious, as time progresses the likelihood of escalation increases [...] The conflict in Ukraine is a genuine threat to European security and world peace as well.[1]

The low-intensity conflict continued in eastern Ukraine for years, but why did it intensify during 2021? Several possible explanations have been given, some speculative. Russia's position in the world economy is weakening as a consequence of a generic move away from fossil fuels. Russia must act now if it wants to remain a superpower. Yet Russia's oil and gas revenues were at an all-time high in 2021 (Statista 2022). The second possible explanation is related to Russian frustration about the failure of years of negotiations. The sense of frustration in diplomacy was apparent in Putin's speeches, but a simple psychological explanation is not helpful either. It seems more plausible to assess the dynamics of the conflict in eastern Ukraine and the development of Ukraine's NATO membership aspirations.

DOI: 10.4324/9781003375326-5
This chapter has been made available under CC-BY-NC-ND 4.0 license.

A possible explanation is that the West's military-technical support for Ukraine strengthened its military so that it was becoming possible for Ukraine to resolve the conflict in Donbas by military means. On the other hand, President Zelenskyy tried to find a solution via negotiations in 2019. The solution would have included OSCE-observed elections in Donetsk and Luhansk and the withdrawal of Russia's unmarked troops. This solution met with fierce domestic resistance in Ukraine, while it was obvious that the state of Ukraine did not have full control over all (para-) military groups fighting against separatists and the Russian forces. When the plan fell apart and the conflict continued, in 2021 Russia started to gather troops near the border, and Zelenskyy started to accelerate Ukraine's NATO membership (corruption was the main barrier to membership). At the same time, NATO organised military exercises close to the Russian border and Ukraine amassed troops alongside the contact line in eastern Ukraine (see Cafruny et al. 2022, 10). The conflict escalated quickly and the risk of war grew alongside it (I reassessed my estimates on the likelihood of the war in late 2021 and early 2022, but apparently not enough).

In August 2021, Zelenskyy's government organised a Crimea forum to return the Crimean peninsula (including Sevastopol) under Ukraine's control.[2] These kinds of developments may have indicated from Russia's point of view that time was running out. It would have to, one way or another, retreat from Ukraine and possibly give up Crimea and accept Ukraine's NATO membership (implying a possible NATO military base in Sevastopol); or it would have to find a way to advance the negotiations based on the Minsk agreement and Ukraine's non-alignment. In this situation, Russia under Putin's leadership took the second option and decided to increase military preparedness at the border. Resorting to coercive diplomacy, it started to demand negotiations with Ukraine and the US (the EU and its member states were seen as less interesting).

In the West, Russia's demands were widely condemned as impossible – and according to a widely circulated phrase "Putin himself knows that his demands are impossible". Moreover, in November 2021, the US and Ukraine signed a Charter on Strategic Partnership, which includes an agreement on Ukraine's entitlement to membership of NATO (Cafruny et al. 2022, 11).

It is difficult for me to see why Ukraine's military non-alignment would have been impossible (cf. the Monroe Doctrine, which the US still follows). According to the OSCE agreements and its concept of equal and indivisible security, the freedom of sovereign states to choose their security arrangements – to decide whether or not to ally and with whom – cannot occur at the expense of others. More generally, the possible and probable consequences of actions must be taken into account. While there was no reason to expect any miraculous improvement in the relations between Russia and the West, at least the conflict in eastern Ukraine could have been resolved through further negotiations and without war had Russia's demands been considered legitimate.

TF: I will start my analysis from the assumption that the implementation of the Minsk agreement could have prevented the war we are facing right now in its current form. In this context, I will not repeat my assessment of what the implementation of the agreement concluded under military pressure would have meant for Ukraine. Suffice it to say that the leaders of Ukraine did not want to implement it the way that Russia interpreted it because they did not believe that the consequences would be desirable in the long term. After 2014, the Ukrainians' trust in Russia and its intentions was lost. The same was true for the wider West as well: France and Germany still tried to facilitate the implementation of the Minsk II agreement because there was no better guarantee of peace in sight. However, the fact that Russia did not acknowledge itself as a party to the conflict was a key problem of the agreement (Åtland 2020; see also Allan & Wolczuk 2022).

Probably sometime in December 2019, the Kremlin concluded that the negotiations concerning the implementation of the Minsk agreement would not proceed in the desired manner. It had already started to give out passports to residents of the separatist areas of east Ukraine. The phase of added military pressure via moving troops to the Ukrainian border did not start before spring 2021. Analysts believed that this operation was Moscow's way to attract attention from new US president Joe Biden, but the corona pandemic may also have caused setbacks in Russia's plans. In spring 2021, tensions between Russia and Ukraine also mounted as a result of an increase in real or alleged incidents on the frontline in eastern Ukraine and because Ukraine decided to cut the main water supply to Crimea. Russia withdrew most of its troops from the Russia–Ukraine border before the summit meeting between Putin and Biden in June, but the military hardware was left in place. The US froze the delivery of its military aid package to Ukraine, but that did not de-escalate the situation. Rather, Ukraine adopted sterner rhetoric against Russia and its occupation of parts of Ukraine (Moshes & Nizhnikau 2022). As Russia's military demonstration did not produce the expected results either directly or via Washington, a new stage began in November of the same year. Simultaneously, the Kremlin raised the stakes by stating that the US and NATO should agree to a legally binding agreement that would prevent NATO enlargement and that

NATO should withdraw its troops and bases from eastern Europe to where they were in 1997.

It would appear that, by December 2021 at the latest, it was more about how large-scale the war was going to be and when it would go ahead, rather than whether it would start at all, and the final decision about the timing and scale of the invasion was probably made at the beginning of February 2022 (see e.g. Risen 2022). To an outside observer, the eruption of a full-scale war was still not obvious as it was not clear whether Putin was merely bluffing and the real focus was on Donbas. The US intelligence community had come to the conclusion that Russia was about to launch a major strategic attack on Ukraine from multiple directions in order to seize most of the country, but neither the Ukrainian nor most of the European allies were convinced that this was the case (Harris et al. 2022). The most compelling reason to believe that Putin was bluffing was that waging war, especially full-scale war, was seen as too great a risk. As the war started, it proved that experts who were sceptical about a full-scale war were not wrong about the magnitude of the risk, but about the Kremlin's assessment of these risks or to what extent it ignored or was willing to take them.

We must beware of reading history backwards and of hindsight bias, meaning that realised outcomes are seen as more likely than they really were (cf. Tetlock 1999; Pohl 2004). Here, the question is not about hindsight bias, however, unless we think that Russia's willingness to take risks or some other factor was affected by the negotiation process that preceded the war. The Kremlin may have believed that the West would bend in the negotiations and hence the war could have been avoided, but the demands presented by the Kremlin and the way the negotiations were carried out seemed more akin to a justification for the war rather than a genuine effort to resolve the conflict.

Why so? The demands that Russia made were maximalist and differed so greatly from previous practice and normative principles that their acceptance would have been humiliating. It is unthinkable that the West would have merely acquiesced to Russia's demands, a country that had blatantly violated international norms before. Such an outcome would have set a precedent after which the West could have found itself on a slippery slope. Not only Ukraine but also external reputation, mutual solidarity, and domestic credibility were at stake. The analogy of Munich in 1938 (see Nyyssönen & Humphreys 2016) was so obvious in light of the security guarantees that Russia was demanding that no key Western politician with any self-respect and career ambition could have accepted them. Much should have been different in a counterfactual sense if Russia's proposal for an agreement had been both accepted and implemented. This does not mean that the Munich analogy has been correctly understood in the West, or that it self-evidently should be a central tenet in the Western political reflection on the lessons of history. Still, it did dictate, rather straightforwardly, the limits of possible international agreements. The Kremlin did not necessarily understand the significance of the Munich analogy for the Western collective memory, but it is still unlikely that the Kremlin truly believed that the West would accept its demands. During Medvedev's term as president, Russia had already proposed a new security agreement, so it was not realistic to expect that the West would be willing to conclude a similar, even more far-reaching security treaty in worsened circumstances. Moreover, Russia did not try to do anything that could have been perceived as a concession by the West, and nor did it attempt to build mutual trust either (rather, it did the opposite), so that the fundamentals of the security treaty could be agreed on. In effect, Russia did not want to negotiate with Ukraine at all.

The West did not want to shoot down Russia's proposals completely, however. Several Western leaders continued the negotiations to the last moment in order to possibly reach a bleak face-saving agreement. Effective behind-the-scenes diplomacy aimed at some kind of reciprocity would have been a solution similar to that of the Cuban crisis, but if face-saving was an issue, the concessions of the West should have been made public. The West primarily offered confidence-building measures and arms control on the basis of reciprocity. We do not know all the details of the negotiations and the possible promises that were made to Russia, but oral reassurances were given that NATO would not expand to Ukraine in any foreseeable future – as German Chancellor Olaf Scholz confirmed to Russian media just over a week before Russia launched its invasion (Harris et al. 2022).

This was not enough for Russia, however. It was not even willing to seriously probe what kind of compromise could have been negotiated with the West (Harris et al. 2022). And why would the legally binding security guarantees it demanded have been a satisfactory solution if Putin did not trust the West, and did not even honour Russia's commitments based on international agreements, such as the Budapest Memorandum? Putin's reassurance about the continuation of the negotiations and his seeming willingness to avoid war, in a situation where actual preparations for war had already got underway, seem grotesque in hindsight.

Negotiations with the West were only one, albeit important, storyline in the run-up to the war. What was even more important was how the Kremlin's perspective on Ukraine systematically shifted – especially in light of public statements and speeches as well as media discourses – towards a view that prepared for and justified a full-scale war. In July 2021, Putin (2021) published a historical essay in which he claimed that Russians and Ukrainians are the same people, basically denying any justification for the existence of a sovereign Ukrainian state. From the Kremlin's point of view, Ukraine was an artificial historical creation and its democratically elected leaders were not legitimate. Ever since the Orange Revolution, state-led Russian media had started to increase its anti-Ukrainian content, but the pace only accelerated after 2014 (Kuzio 2017; Khaldarova 2021). Groundless claims made in December 2021 about genocide in east Ukraine, Ukraine's plans for acquiring nuclear weapons or harbouring American chemical laboratories that were developing weapons intended for use against ethnic Russians belong to the same framing. A state that unleashes this kind of misinformation on the public cannot negotiate in good faith.

The question that remains is the extent to which the Kremlin itself believed in the propagandist image of Ukraine it had created and was used as a justification of the war (Putin 2022). It surely believed that there were nationalistic forces in Ukraine that had formed their identity in opposition to Russia and that discriminated against Russian speakers, but the allegation of genocide in Donbas, for which the Kremlin could not provide any evidence, was a pretext that mainly served the purpose of justifying the war to the domestic audience. Russia was not ready to defend its claim about genocide in eastern Ukraine at the International Court of Justice. In the same vein, the Kremlin's allegation that Ukrainians are led by Nazis is most likely a symbolic marker for domestic and international audiences, rather than a real concern to be taken literally. Despite their nuclear deterrence, Russians may have believed in the possibility that Russia could be taken by surprise someday, similarly to the Soviet Union when Germany attacked in 1941, although such a threat would not have been seen as imminent. However, when launching the war on Ukraine, Russia was ready to weaken its western defence bordering the NATO countries. The expansion of NATO was a concern for the Kremlin, raised vehemently on many occasions, but was it more of a profound irritation or did the Kremlin genuinely believe that Ukraine could become a member of NATO one day, and that Russia might have to give up its military base in Crimea? The fact that the West regarded NATO as a defensive alliance, and did not believe that Russia faced any major military threat from outside in any case because of its nuclear arsenal, did not mean that the Kremlin thought the same way (see Tsygankov 2018).

Whatever the case, Russian short- or mid-term worries about Ukrainian membership in NATO were not justified: the prospect was hardly any closer in 2021 than it was in 2008. There was no evidence that Biden's regime would have advocated any swift NATO enlargement towards Ukraine. On the contrary, Biden turned down Zelenskyy's wishes for Ukraine's NATO membership in any foreseeable future and stated that the country was still too corrupt to gain admission to the Membership Action Plan. The US did provide military assistance for Ukraine after 2014, but it was worth less than 10% of Ukraine's defence budget. It included military training and some defensive weapons such as anti-tank missiles, but no long-range weaponry. Multinational military drills in western Ukraine in 2021 involved only 6,000 troops, while at the same time Russia and Belarus exercised with almost 200,000 troops close to the Ukrainian border.

Russian leaders may have believed that Ukraine's Western orientation had to be stopped before it was too late, but the paradox is that the Kremlin also believed in the decline of the West. The mutual security guarantees of NATOs article 5 was often ridiculed as an empty promise. The US withdrawal from Afghanistan ostensibly strengthened the Kremlin's beliefs about the West's resolve, but at the same time it exaggerated the Western involvement in Ukraine. Another paradox is that Ukrainian public opinion did not support NATO membership before Russia's annexation of Crimea.

More than any possible NATO enlargement towards Ukraine, the Kremlin's fear may have been fuelled by the fact that a sovereign, democratic, and prosperous Ukraine would set an example to the Russian people, which might diminish the position of the leaders in the Kremlin (see Duncan 2013; Pankow & Patman 2018; Person & McFaul 2022). At least the Kremlin was convinced that the West had played an active part in the colour revolutions and that the West harboured plans for regime change in Russia. Western leaders never succeeded in fully conveying the message that when criticising the Kremlin for its suppression of the opposition, it was not taking a stance against the Kremlin, but rather for democratic institutions. Even if the chances of a protest movement from below being able to oust Putin and his associates from the Kremlin were minimal in the advent of the war, the fear of a domestic revolution may have been real.

The decision to start a full-scale war and the developments that led to it lend more plausibility to the interpretation that Russia's actions were guided not by fear, but by identity-based neo-imperialistic motives to control areas that were once part of the Soviet Union or Russian Empire. The politics of history that glorifies past war success and denies atrocities, geopolitical thinking that draws on great-power nostalgia, and a conservative shift in values since the beginning of Putin's third term in 2012 all seem to justify this interpretation. Putin's comparison between himself and Peter the Great as a leader who takes back territories and reinforces Russia is in line with this neo-imperial motivation for expansion (Tharoor 2022). Status may also have mattered, but probably not Russia's position in relation to the US, but rather the status hierarchy in relation to Ukraine and the contempt towards disloyal weaker states, and the need to punish the nation and its leaders who dared to challenge Russia's position. Whether fear, greed, status, or revenge, with our existing knowledge no definitive answer can be given, especially as all of these motives might have been deeply entangled in the spiral that led to war (cf. Lebow 2010b).

Russia's excessive war aims indicate, I think, that after 2014 it was no longer about what Ukraine did to prevent the war, but about restraining its sovereignty and accepting Moscow's dominance. Ukrainians could have kept their nominal status as an independent state, but they would have needed to choose political leaders loyal to Moscow and the country would have been integrated more tightly into the Russian *mir*, rather than remaining neutral between Russia and the West. Widespread corruption in Ukraine and the political influence and violent acts of far-right groups were a concern in the West as well, and Moscow's tutelage would hardly have improved transparency in Ukraine. On the other hand, these were claimed causes among myriad others, including risible ones. Patriarch Kirill of Moscow, for example, regarded so-called decadent values such as pride parades as a justification for the war (see Moscow Times 2022). How much Western aid Ukraine received to boost its defence, whether its army became more capable or not, whether it organised an international conference to discuss ways of returning the Crimean peninsula to Ukraine, or whether it announced its willingness to join NATO more eagerly than before are all secondary issues that would have probably only affected the timing of the war at most. The same goes for the actions of the West. Leadership changes in the West, the retreat from Afghanistan, internal divisions caused by right-wing populism, and pressure created by the pandemic might have reinforced the Kremlin's perspective on the correct time for action, but even then the question is not about whether the war would start, but rather when.

Why then did Russia embark on a full-scale war despite the massive risks on the battlefield, in domestic politics, and with regard to foreign relations? Irrespective of how great the possible gains from the war were estimated by the Kremlin, its willingness to take a risk had clearly increased since 2014. Possible explanations can be found in diverse psychological theories (Forsberg & Pursiainen 2017). According to prospect theory, the willingness to take risks increases if the actor in question perceives that its position is weakening.[3] The threshold for taking a risk may also have been lowered because of the groupthink that was forming when the leadership circle became smaller and more exclusive in the Kremlin, leading to overconfidence and a lack of critical thinking. Some deeply ingrained emotions that were highly typical of the Russian leaders such as frustration or anger, not to mention resentment, can also lead to risk-taking. Moreover, it cannot be ruled out that Putin's personality may have changed because of his long tenure as leader, and perhaps even because of the coronavirus isolation before the war, which reduced his contacts to a minimum. The same factors can explain misjudgements: the leaders in the Kremlin simply did not have a correct picture of the risks of a full-scale war. Putin seemed to believe that the military campaign would be swift and successful: he had already boasted in 2014 that he could take Kiev in two weeks if he wanted (see e.g. Traynor 2014). So far, the effects of such psychological mechanisms are speculative, based on proven theories and second-hand information. Hopefully, we can give more accurate answers drawing on more systematic empirical evidence sometime in the future.

HP: We agree that the implementation of the Minsk agreement could have prevented the war on its current large scale, although your formulation seems to ignore the importance of the question of NATO expansion. I can well understand why in this situation (Russia attacking Ukraine and bombing its cities, also killing civilians) you want to use ethically loaded terms to describe Russia and its actions – "grotesque", "blatant", and so on – but this tendency may reinforce the essentialism that I mentioned earlier. Following a well-known metaphor, I think a peace researcher should assume, first and foremost, the role of a doctor rather than a judge and analyse causes and processes even when the aim is also to expand the scope of the rule of law and democracy in world politics (the rule of law implies the possibility of convictions and sentencing; see Patomäki 2001). I continue to think that you tend to ignore the issue of double standards and demand something from Russia that you do not expect from those Western actors who have participated in one-sided accusations and unilateral military interventions that tend to erode the legitimacy of international law.[4]

On the other hand, I do not disagree with all of your interpretations. The antagonisation and radicalisation of interpretations are part of conflict dynamics. Earlier, I argued that identities, preferences and the like are not so much "revealed" as constructed through inter- and intra-actions. In the reproductive and transformative processes of social interactions, various layers of history are present, many processes are path-dependent, and causation tends to be cumulative. The recent inclinations of Putin and members of his government to resort to neo-imperialistic rhetoric are fully compatible with the substance of my previous analysis. The government of Bush Jr and the events of 9/11 opened up space for competing neo-imperialisms and it was only a matter of time before the same rhetoric would start to spread and become common, in its specific way in each context. I am not a Kremlinologist nor have I spent much time analysing Putin's texts. To the extent that there is nostalgia for the tsars or the Soviet Empire, it is no more justified than nostalgia for the British (cf. Brexit) or French empires. The time for such empires is over.

On the one hand, you maintain that it does seem that by December 2021, at the latest, it was more about how widespread the war was going to be and when it would start, rather than whether it would start at all. Leaving aside the precise timing (indeed, the decision to invade might have been made already by November or December 2021), your claim overlooks the process where Ukraine, the US, and parts of the EU were active participants, and where Russia was practically told that its security interests are not legitimate and that its concerns need not be taken seriously. You mention, however, that several Western leaders continued negotiations to reach "a bleak face-saving agreement". You do not specify the substance of this "bleak agreement". Your bold suggestion that "after 2014 it was no longer about what Ukraine did to prevent the war, but about restraining its sovereignty and accepting Moscow's dominance" does not correspond to the actual agenda of the negotiations. It seems to me that what you call a "bleak agreement" would have in fact excluded Russia's central demands: prevention of Ukraine's NATO membership and implementation of the Minsk II agreement. What logic is there in responses such as: "we do not accept your demands {a,b,c}, because you are really pursuing aims {x,y,z}"? While {x,y,z} may be unacceptable, it does not mean that reasonable demands {a,b,c} cannot be discussed. If there is no trust and the demands of the opposing party are not considered real or serious, negotiations will become next to impossible.

You argue that "the demands that Russia made were maximalist and differed so greatly from previous conventions and normative principles that their acceptance would have been humiliating". By "maximalist demands" you seem to refer to those American weapon systems that were to be removed from areas close to Russian borders (cf. our earlier discussion on the Monroe Doctrine)? But does your point on "humiliation" mean that the problem concerned "saving face" on the Western side as well? If so, it reinforces my point concerning a certain symmetry of the situation, including the fact that both sides were unable to change their policies.

At any rate, the following statement seems to be a somewhat careless rhetorical move:

> How much Western aid Ukraine received to boost its defence, whether its army became more capable or not, whether it organised an international conference to discuss ways of returning the Crimean Peninsula to Ukraine, or whether it announced its willingness to join NATO more eagerly than before are all secondary issues that would have probably only affected the timing of the war at most.

You seem to assume that, in reality, Russia had decided to start the war irrespective of the negotiations and their outcomes. I cannot rule this possibility out completely but, as far as I can see, no evidence to back up your claim has emerged to date. There is, however, the danger of circular reasoning: first, the *ego* refuses to negotiate issues that the other side claims to be decisive ("here is the red line" and so on), and then, when the *alter* implements its pronounced threats and responds with aggression, the ego interprets this as proof that negotiations in good faith would have been in vain. Moreover, somewhat at odds with what you are saying, it seems to me that this line of reasoning stems from the certainty-of-hindsight bias, which is the "tendency to slip into viewing what happened as retrospectively inevitable by quickly forgetting how uncertain they once were about what would happen" (Tetlock 1999, 341). Finally, it appears somewhat contradictory to say that (1) the implementation of the Minsk II agreement could have prevented the war in Ukraine, and (2) Russia would have attacked Ukraine irrespective of the outcome of the negotiations, which also concerned issues related to the Minsk II agreement.

Anyhow, in January 2022 I concluded that, as Ukraine and the West had refused to negotiate the issues that were declared decisive by Russia, Putin's government found itself cornered (in part this corner was of its own making, against the advice of classical political realists on wise diplomacy). An empty-handed retreat would have meant humiliation for Putin's government – the only remaining option being the escalation of the war in eastern Ukraine. Even though I was acutely aware of this, I underestimated the likelihood of a full-scale invasion because I thought – like many other experts, as you too indicate – that the risks were huge. Indeed, the failure of judgement seemed to lie in thinking that Russia's leadership agreed with this risk assessment. Here, the (social) psychological theories you emphasise may have real explanatory power.[5] You also mention that the willingness to take risks increases if the actor in question perceives that its position is weakening, and I gave a couple of reasons why Russia's position could have been perceived as weakening (Ukraine strengthening its military capabilities, the Crimea forum, and so on, and you have in fact continued this list). I am not an expert in military issues, but a force of 150,000 troops seemed back then, and still seems, inadequate for conquering a country the size of Ukraine, even given the surprise effect, more powerful technological capabilities, and likely air superiority. Added to this, such a war incurs massive costs in economic and political terms (this would have been the case even without the unprecedented scale of sanctions). The war has been going on for over half a year now, and it seems that this risk assessment was on the mark.[6]

TF: Your comment seems to be linked to whether I interpret Russia according to different standards compared to the West. The issue is also whether the demands Russia made were reasonable or legitimate, and whether the West should therefore have accepted them. I do think that the reasons that the West had for its actions, or rather non-actions, before the full-scale war were more justifiable than those of Russia, but even if the West had conceded to Russia's demands about NATO, Russia would have probably started the war against Ukraine in any case after the implementation of the Minsk agreement failed. The implementation of the Minsk agreement was not one of the demands that Russia presented to the West, so I do not see that my argument about the secondary role of these negotiations with the West and their more central role with regard to the Minsk agreement as contradictory.

When I say that the West could not agree to Russia's demands because it would have been humiliating, I primarily mean that it was the West's self-perception, but I also believe that the Kremlin perceived it similarly: it felt that it had been humiliated in the past and now it was the West's turn. "Maximalism" may be a poor choice of concept because, from Russia's point of view, the demands might have been closer to some "minimalist" requisites for its ideal world, but Russia seemed to increase its demands during the negotiation process rather than decrease them in the hope of an agreement. Nevertheless, the West was willing to discuss all of the reasonable concerns that Russia raised, including its ideas of indivisible security, while the German and French leaders in particular were seeking a compromise, and there is enough evidence that Russia was disinterested in pursuing that path further (e.g. Harris et al. 2022). Moreover, I do not think that there was symmetry in the bargaining positions of the parties because Russia was clearly the demandeur. Russia's humiliation was not at stake here in the same way as the West's because it would have gained at least something from the negotiations and the Russian media could have easily depicted the outcome as a victory if Putin had so wished. Of course, there is no certainty about what would have happened if the West had conceded to all or most of Russia's demands. Yet the view about Russia having a preference for war rather than negotiations is not merely a result of hindsight bias. I was of the opinion that the Russian demands looked like a pretext for war rather than a genuine attempt to negotiate a solution, even in December 2021 (see Taskinen 2021).

You also seem to assume that I would not draw similar conclusions about the actions of the US, for example, if the evidence were the same as for Russia's actions now. This argument would be a viable criticism if I were wrong about Russia, but if my bias led me to interpret the US in too lenient a manner, it would not debunk my interpretation of the causes of the war in Ukraine. We should not analyse world politics through the prism of the Cold War in which the US sets the standard for our assessment of Russia. As our discussion is not about how we explain wars started by the US or other Western actors, I can only respond by saying that I have had no difficulty in being critical of decisions to use military power in Kosovo, Iraq, or Libya, for example. To be sure, the West does not always negotiate in good faith. For example, in the Rambouillet negotiations that preceded the Kosovo War, the Western leaders might have well known that the ultimatum presented to Yugoslavia was such that the Serb leader, Slobodan Milosevic, could not accept it.

You also had a remark about language. As a researcher, I try to avoid words that are normatively loaded. However, I felt that the genre of this discussion is one in which they could fit. We cannot completely avoid normatively loaded language even in the scientific genre, but as critical realists we should use those words that are most accurate even if they are normatively loaded (Bhaskar 1979, 75). Using words like "ruthless" to describe the character or actions of some other leaders such as Donald Trump does not feel like an exaggeration either.

HP: An alternative interpretation is that Russia was not getting an agreement on anything, and thus raised the stakes by means of threats (coercive diplomacy) and bigger demands, in the hope of being taken more seriously. Obviously that did not help, and Putin found himself cornered instead. Be the truth about the immediate pre-war demands as it may (hopefully empirical evidence about the insider discussions in the Kremlin will emerge one day), let me make a very brief comment on normatively loaded language. I remember the passage you mention from Bhaskar well. It is based on a famous example given by Isaiah Berlin comparing different accounts of what happened under Nazi rule: (1) "the country was depopulated"; (2) "millions of people died"; (3) "millions of people were killed"; (4) "millions of people were massacred". Bhaskar argued that while all four statements are true, (4) is not only the most evaluative, it is also the most precise and accurate.

I agree that language is evaluative (see also Sayer 2011). Moreover, the claim that science and scholarship must be neutral and impartial is not a fact in itself but a *normative* requirement, which is closely related to the *regulative metaphor* of truth understood as a correspondence to the way things really are in the world. On the other hand, it is also precisely because epistemological relativism prevails that science and scholarship should be as neutral and impartial as possible. It is beyond reasonable doubt that the Nazis adopted and implemented systematic policies of mass murder (these included the 1942 Final Solution to the Jewish Question), but most of the things we have been discussing here are not beyond reasonable doubt – as testified by our interpretative disagreements and, in many instances, by the lack of solid empirical evidence.

Violent conflicts generate a particular context for scholarship. As I have argued elsewhere (Patomäki 2001, 732, especially note 8), in many such contexts it must be the task of the peace researcher to build consensus by drawing on shared background assumptions, or to devise compromise settlements in peace negotiations or some such. In other contexts, emancipation nevertheless requires the starting of dissensus. A clash of interpretations or *ortodoxas* originates in conceptions of identity, actions, and history that are buried deep within "self-evident" assumptions and related reifications and mystifications. Both tasks – consensus-building and critical analysis of the prevailing stories and their "self-evident" assumptions – require the avoidance of overly loaded evaluative language based on the idea that one side of the conflict is good and the other bad. A critical stance does not mean that we cannot attribute moral or legal responsibility for this invasion or any other wrongdoing, but it does mean that we must adopt a hypothetical attitude and be careful about respecting the norms of neutrality and impartiality in describing and explaining what has happened.

Notes

1 See https://patomaki.fi/2016/12/venaja-keskustelusta-osa-2-tulevaisuuden-vaaroja-voidaan-arvioida-jarkiperaisesti/.
2 Forty-five countries took part altogether. For the aims of the forum, see https://crimea-platform.org/en/about.

3 In April 2021, I wrote with Christer Pursiainen about prospect theory's predictive power: "Let us consider our above example of Putin's risk-taking vis-à-vis Ukraine from this perspective. We could speculate that if during the prolonged Ukrainian conflict Putin will, for instance, perceive that Ukraine had incrementally edged closer to NATO membership, that would put Putin again in the domain of loss. This would then lead to a more assertive and risk-seeking policy by Russia, which would be likely to escalate the conflict or start an open war against Kiev" (Pursiainen & Forsberg 2021, 107).

4 You write "Groundless claims made in December 2021 about genocide in East Ukraine and the Ukrainians harbouring American chemical laboratories that were developing weapons intended for use against ethnic Russians belong to the same framing. A state that unleashes this kind of misinformation on the public cannot negotiate in good faith". We have heard similar kinds of false claims from Western state actors in the context of, say, Kosovo and Iraq, but my conclusion is *not* that "we" cannot negotiate with the US, UK, or France in good faith. Rather, the critique of spreading disinformation or violating international law applies to everyone.

5 Soon after the attack, some tentative evidence emerged that group thinking and consequent organisational stupidity, typical of hierarchical organisations, had affected Russia's decision. The information that reaches the top group of "yes men" tends to be biased. "Yes men" conform with the group thinking and avoid raising controversial issues or alternative solutions. It seems that the department of the Russian intelligence service that was responsible for Ukraine feared Putin's and his inner circle's reaction – or even wrath – and produced information that they wanted to hear. Based on this information and their own preconceptions, the inner circle seems to have expected that a disorganised, corrupt, and weak Ukraine would fall quickly.

6 I am inclined to agree with Norman Angell (1909) that in a modern interdependent world, all interstate wars are irrational. Even wars that merely aim at temporary control, like the wars in Afghanistan or Iraq, become so costly that they eventually fail. Russia has also had similar experiences, albeit on a smaller scale.

6 The Shape of Things to Come

TF: It was March 2022 when we originally wrote this dialogue in Finnish. Then, as now, the outcome of the war in Ukraine is difficult to predict. My judgement then was that, at best, the war could subside after a ceasefire in a matter of a few weeks, but that it could also last for a long time, even for years. If Russia does not reassess its war aims and leave Ukraine and Ukraine does not collapse – and that is unlikely as long as the West is providing Ukraine with military and other assistance – we are hardly going to see any swift changes on the battlefield. At the time of this writing, the Ukrainian counteroffensive has succeeded in retaking towns and land areas both in the south and in the north from the Russian troops, but it is too early to call this as a turning point that would lead to a Russian withdrawal from Ukraine. A long war of attrition still seems likely, as there are no signs that the parties could agree on a ceasefire. Before the massacre and atrocities of Bucha became evident, there was perhaps a small window of opportunity to call a halt to the war, but the negotiations did not really take off, mainly because Russia was not genuinely interested in them, and there have been no serious diplomatic efforts to end the war since then. However, the war could reach a stalemate during the course of the year, transforming it into a more low-intensity conflict, as before the invasion. The war can still end in a victory for Russia, but it is exhausting its resources needed for continuing its offensive effectively. Moreover, it is unlikely that Russia can effectively control wide areas of Ukraine, so the conflict could continue at a low intensity even if Russia declared victory. The war could also end in defeat for Russia, but that would require a change of power in the Kremlin, as it is difficult to imagine a Russia led by Putin and his associates admitting to having lost the war.

It is hard to see how a durable peace could be negotiated at the moment. Russia does not appear to have abandoned any of its wider goals of securing territorial annexations in eastern Ukraine and Crimea, possibly by creating a land bridge in southern Ukraine, duly changing the regime and establishing de facto control of Ukraine's foreign and security policy, including its demilitarisation. Russia has not clearly stated its minimal goals or conditions for a peace deal. However, any peace deal would require more concessions from Russia than a simple acceptance of the legitimacy of Ukraine's current government and recognition of its borders, at least along the frontline. First and foremost, Russia's demand for the demilitarisation of Ukraine is unrealistic, as it started the war. Ukraine could accept a deal that it will remain neutral but that is hardly the key to a solution. From a gritty realist perspective, Ukraine could agree to losses of territory in Crimea and eastern Ukraine that were controlled by Russia and the separatists before the invasion. So far, the Ukrainians have not been willing to discuss such concessions and it is not clear whether an agreement based on the 2014 frontline would satisfy Russia in any case. Moreover, it is difficult to overlook the issue of war crimes and war reparations, and hence any agreement will be much more difficult than before the war.[1]

If Russia's military success does not allow it to set the peace conditions, a peace deal would require some visible reciprocity or trust that the war would not erupt again. This is not likely to happen as long as Putin's Russia denies Ukraine's right to full sovereignty. From the Ukrainian perspective, Russia is only ready for temporary concessions: a ceasefire or an armistice in order to gather strength and consolidate the annexation of the occupied territories. However, the war may subside without any formal peace agreement or cessation of hostilities when the parties deem that they cannot achieve any significant strategic advances by military force, and when other domestic concerns require more attention. It is of course also possible that the war will escalate even further, and the danger of the use of nuclear weapons cannot be ruled out.

HP: Thanks for your reasonable viewpoints. Let me start my response with a few methodological remarks. As Philip Tetlock (2005) has argued based on systematic empirical research, political disagreements among experts are systematic and characteristically also concern – often especially – rationally justifiable beliefs about the future. The problem is not only that the capacity of experts to predict the future in open systems that are characterised by open-endedness and uncertainty is poor; a deeper problem is that partisans rarely admit error even in the face of massive evidence. There is, however, a significant difference between hedgehog and fox strategies in approaching the problem of anticipation. Many follow the hedgehog strategy of dogged persistence: "know one big thing", toil devotedly within one tradition, and reach for formulaic solutions to ill-defined problems. Foxes prefer eclectic cunning: "know many little things", draw from an eclectic array of traditions, and accept ambiguity and contradiction as inevitable. Foxes are better at learning from mistakes. A self-critical, dialectical style of reasoning can spare experts many mistakes. I think we both prefer, at least in principle, the fox orientation. However, the fox strategy involves pitfalls as well. One is the potential lack of consistency: one draws too freely from sources based on contradictory assumptions, or too much likelihood is assigned to too many scenarios. The second is that "trendy open-mindedness [often] looks like old-fashioned confusion" (Tetlock 2005, 23), not least because all possibilities are covered – and the sum total of likelihoods may even exceed one.

Like many others, I underestimated the likelihood of a full-scale invasion of Ukraine (as discussed above in Chapter 5). I am not an expert on military matters and, even if I were, there is too much uncertainty about the situation in Ukraine in September 2022 to develop consistent and adequate scenarios, and to assign plausible probabilities to them. Moreover, many scenarios I have seen are based on guesswork and speculation about unknowables, such as what does this or that individual or collective actor "really think" (non-publicly) at the moment – or will possibly think in the near future? Somewhat more reasonably, we could engage in counting actual and potential resources and try to calculate prospects in a war of attrition (cf. e.g. Vershinin 2022). However, these resources are not only determined by production capabilities but depend to a large degree on ethical and political constraints, and reflections on them. Russia's production capacities are much bigger than Ukraine's and remain mostly intact, the main problem for Russia being those military hardware components that they need to import (population ratio is 140/40 million, Russia's GDP/capita is considerably higher than Ukraine's, thus Russia's GDP is 10+ times bigger, and so on).

What seems clear is that the Russian leadership face major technical and political constraints. Russia can allocate only a part of its military resources to Ukraine (with 20,000+ kilometres of borders and large areas to guard, and a military presence also outside of Russia). So far (until late summer 2022), the Kremlin has been careful in relying on contracted personnel from the remote and poor rural areas of the vast Russian territory, often from Siberia. It seems that this is a conscious strategy to avoid the "Vietnam effect" of its citizens turning against the war, especially in major cities such as Moscow and St. Petersburg. The Western military support for Ukraine has been considerable and, in some cases, this support has already partly depleted their stores. From a methodological perspective, the NATO support means that the

"Ukrainian capacity" is incalculable to the extent that a key part of it depends on decisions made by NATO countries, which consider competing priorities, assess risks, and ponder ethics. Moreover, the overall situation is dynamic. For instance, for the Russian leadership, conventional escalation would be costly politically as they would have to declare war and start to mobilise their reserves (again the risk of a "Vietnam effect"); yet a long war of attrition or serious losses can undermine the legitimacy of the Putin regime (perhaps especially vis-à-vis the hawks).

I am therefore inclined to discuss the near future in normatively oriented terms by assessing the best- and worst-case scenarios at a rather abstract level. Later, I will relate this analysis to building long-term and large-scale scenarios about possible global futures. Prima facie, the best-case scenario concerns de-escalation and a negotiated agreement capable of stopping the violence and destruction in Ukraine. All wars come to an end. In the absence of an outright victory by one side or the other, or total destruction of the world, all violent conflicts or wars end in a reciprocally negotiated agreement. It is not a matter of whether there will be an agreement, but rather *when* and with *what contents*. From one perspective, "the issue is how to revert from an unconstrained and militarised conflict to one that is regulated in a more civilised manner" (Krause 2019, 923). Both politics and war are characterised by conflicts. Figure 6.1 illustrates how politics can change and be transformed into violence in some contexts K_i (Transformation 1), and how violence in contexts K_j can change and be transformed into politics (Transformation 2).

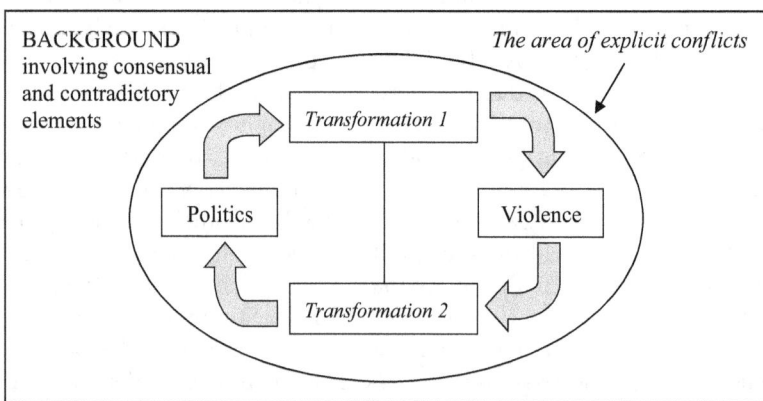

Figure 6.1 Politics and violence.

Social activity and inter-activity are always linked with certain background assumptions based on a common understanding, and these are considered self-evident – or not even noticed – by the agents. Even when A and B struggle violently against each other, they can share a number of the same, similar, or analogical background assumptions. Public disagreements nevertheless require conscious public airing. Politics and violence both fall within the area of conscious, purposeful conflicts. The most acute problem of transforming violence into politics and diplomacy concerns Ukraine, but the real issue is more general. You are right about the current situation (no ongoing peace negotiations) and I agree partly with your interpretation about why this may be the case (e.g. the role of atrocities in Bucha and other places). My point is rather that there are good reasons to encourage the parties to negotiate through various initiatives, offers to mediate or facilitate, and so forth. Now the US, and the West more generally, seem to be pushing for more war.

Moreover, the public affairs (*res publica*) stemming from the interconnectedness of Russia with the rest of the world will not disappear because of this war. Sanctions and countersanctions vis-à-vis Russia indicate that what we see is not some sort of ideal-typical Cold War world of two separate camps, but a world of complex interdependence. This interdependence shapes regional and worldwide relations and processes, for example through value chains, the overlap between different national jurisdictions, networks of informational and financial exchange, the regional and global formation of aggregate efficient demand, and so on. As a result of regressive developments since the 1990s, this interdependence has now become increasingly weaponised, also vis-à-vis China and others, and vice versa, with China and Russia as active participants (see Farrell & Newman 2019). In other words, interdependence has been subjected to halfway transformation 1. The weaponisation of interdependence tends to hurt everyone over time. This gives even more reasons to think that the task of transformation 2 awaits us, whether we like it or not. Communication and cooperation must be the aim also in this wider context, rather than the further inflaming of antagonisms.

The worst-case scenario concerns the escalation of the war. When considering the emotional nature of the war, the current level of weaponisation of interdependence, and the dynamics of the war itself, in my cautious assessment escalation of the conflict seems more likely than the scenario of the war dragging on for a long time. Escalation could eventually even lead to a nuclear war between Russia and NATO. Even if that likelihood remains slim, the best assessment we can make about it can only be based on (inter)subjective judgements of Bayesian or Keynesian probability. Typically, risk is measured as the expected value of the loss (risk = [probability of E happening] x [expected loss in case of E]). This of course presupposes that we can express all the consequences in the same units, such as money, which is not true in the case of a nuclear war. How could we measure the loss of billions of lives and the collapse of industrial civilisation – not to mention the possibility of the total destruction of the human world? Assuming that the value of the loss of nuclear war is infinite (even if nothing is literally infinite in the universe), in rational decision-making – especially if we follow the maximin rule – any course of action is always better than that which increases the risk of a nuclear war even slightly. The only rational course of action would be to work towards a world where the possibility of an immediate or all-out nuclear war is zero. We could of course elaborate upon this analysis and try to break the problem into smaller parts, but there is a further consideration that must be mentioned here, namely the so-called precautionary principle. As in the context of climate change, where there are threats of very serious or irreversible damage, a lack of full scientific certainty about the possibilities and probabilities should not be used as a reason for postponing precautionary measures, but rather we should confront the reality of uncertainty in the form of known unknowns and genuine surprise (see Derbyshire & Morgan 2022).

TF: When you say that the best option is to de-escalate and negotiate an agreement, the question revolves around how we can achieve de-escalation and a negotiated agreement. To suggest that the West should not provide Ukraine with military assistance is a very hollow guideline: it would still not stop the war and make Russia de-escalate accordingly. The war's logic has not been one of mutual escalation reminiscent of the spiral model, as Russia has had escalation dominance the whole time: it has deployed more troops and heavier weapons than Ukraine and used them in a manner that is likely to escalate rather than de-escalate the conflict. Yet we cannot be sure whether the deterrence model applies to the relations between Russia and Ukraine either (Jervis 1976, ch. 3). It seems that the West's attempt to employ deterrence not by denial but by punishment, namely threatening with political and economic countermeasures should Russia invade Ukraine, failed badly.

That wars end through negotiations is trivially true, unless we talk about total annihilation or some sort of waning with time, but the Western scholars and pundits who suggest negotiations do not have very much of substance to say about how such negotiations would restore a just or durable peace. Rather, their advice is easy to regard as the art of "Westsplaining", where the Ukrainians' own subjectivity is denounced and the conflict is seen simply as one between Russia and the West (Mälksoo 2022). It is illusionary to think that going back to Putin's demands in December 2021, such as Ukraine's neutrality, would restore peace.[2]

In order for peace negotiations to be successful, the old wisdom is that the conflict should first have reached some level of ripeness that has the characteristics of a "mutually hurting stalemate" (Zartman 2001). To the extent that a mutually hurting stalemate involves subjective perceptions, we are far from it but, having said that, subjective perceptions can also change relatively quickly. The problem is that both sides currently seem to think that time is on their side: the Ukrainians believe that Putin is terminally ill and will die soon, or that some other political change in the Kremlin will take place, while the Russians believe that the West will not continue to support Ukraine for long, and Russia's victory can then be secured thanks to its military superiority. In any case, achieving such a stalemate has become more not less likely because of Western military assistance to Ukraine.

Even if the spiral model did not apply, the danger of military escalation to a nuclear conflict cannot be entirely ruled out. Yet it is also part of Russian tactics to give the impression that such an escalation is in the playbook. Although Russia's nuclear doctrine refers to an existential threat, some Russian representatives and pundits started to argue that a preemptive nuclear strike is possible if Russia's victory in Ukraine is denied, while Putin used to be more reassuring that nuclear weapons would not be used (see e.g. Trevelyan 2022). Nuclear talk may be irresponsible but Russia may have seen that it works to the extent that the West takes it into consideration (Sussex 2022). So far, the fear of nuclear warfare has restrained the West: it has not intervened directly in the conflict and has not condoned Ukraine using Western arms in strikes on Russian territory.

The West has been wary of escalation. It has not opened any new fronts or delivered types of weapons that Russia would not have already used. The risk that providing heavy armoury to Ukraine would escalate into a nuclear war has been assessed as not so high that the West should refrain from it, despite many warnings. If Ukraine started to intensify its operations in the Russian territory, the situation might change and lead to new assessments in the West. Although the West aims at weakening Russia's capability of waging war, a poor and internally fragile Russia is not in the interests of the West.

Irrespective of the precise outcome of the war, the conflict between Russia and the West is likely to become a long and languishing new Cold War (or whatever term will be invented for the new era of the relationship). It is unclear as to what extent the rules and norms of the old Cold War will apply in the new circumstances, as concepts such as deterrence and containment depend on the context. The new Cold War is not an ideological conflict, even though Russia has tried to present itself as the protector of traditional values against the decadent and liberal West. The West is more unified than expected at the start of the war. It perceives itself as the champion of the ideals of liberal democracy and the protector of the liberal world order, but cracks can appear in this unity, even serious ones, as the domestic politics of the US has been shaky and polarised.

However, compared to the situation after World War II, the new Cold War with Russia is significantly more asymmetric: this does not make managing the conflict and resolving issues any easier; on the contrary, reciprocity might be more difficult to achieve. The Russian military has underperformed in the Ukrainian War and it will take time before its striking capability can be restored to the previous level. Even at full strength, there is no comparison to the Soviet military might during the Cold War. For that reason, some cracks in the Western unity may not immediately change the balance, and the West can afford some of those. The main threat to the West from Russia is not its conventional capabilities per se, but its "brutality, appetite for risk and nuclear weapons" (Dalsjö et al. 2022, 22). As a consequence of the war, the Kremlin has become even more bigoted and repressive than before, and the unpredictability of its actions has increased.

I do not want to sound too pessimistic, but without a regime change in Russia, a new cooperative and rule-based security order cannot be rebuilt during the lifetime of our generation. We have seen some signs of dissatisfaction in the Russian political elite, but Putin's popularity has remained broad. Any new leader will have a difficult start both in domestic and international politics. One of the saddest repercussions of the war is that it will negatively affect the images of the younger generations who are now at a formative age and for whom the collective memory of the Cold War was already very distant. As long as the present regime in Russia remains in power, the West should settle for containing Russia as it did after World War II, and believe that the momentum for change will eventually come (cf. Kennan 1947; Meister 2022). People-to-people cooperation will not be any panacea for change but, in my view, it is in the interests of the West to allow for such contacts rather than restrict them too much. People-to-people contacts are more important for the future than for any immediate change. It will be a challenge for the West to recognise when more institutional cooperation with Russia can be resumed on the basis of mutual trust, because some people and states will likely set the bar unreasonably high. In any case, Russia will also have its own will and say in the future, and conflicts of interest with the West will remain. Yet when the preconditions for restoring the relations exist, hopefully, the then leaders will be open-minded and bold so that they can firstly seize the moment, and duly not allow the history after the end of the Cold War to repeat itself.

Russia has aimed at changing the whole world order. Such a change may come about in any case, independently of the war in Ukraine, but it will not necessarily make Russia any stronger. It may just become more dependent on China. Russia's invasion of Ukraine was widely condemned in the United Nations, but the old "Third World" has not joined the West in sanctioning and isolating Russia. Rather, they have refrained from participating in the conflict and have tried to benefit from the clash as much as they can, although the war may have consequences such as a food crisis, which will affect them directly. Very few countries are wholeheartedly supporting Russia, but many are sceptical about the West and indifferent to questions of justice in the conflict. The future role of China in the world order is pivotal: it is dependent on the Western world markets, but it cannot abandon Russia. Predictions that China would immediately see that it now has the chance to increase its pressure on Taiwan and launch a military operation to seize it have thus far been too alarmist. Moreover, the war may also offer many other countries, such as India, new possibilities to raise their profile. India has also become more attractive to Russia, as closer relations with it may help to reduce its dependence on China.

HP: My point is that the US, and the West more generally, seem to be pushing for more war, instead of encouraging the Ukrainians to engage in peace negotiations. This point has no direct bearing on the question of sending military equipment and other forms of aid to Ukraine. Article 51 of the UN Charter states:

> nothing in the present Charter shall impair the inherent right of individual or collective self-defence if an armed attack occurs against a Member of the United Nations until the Security Council has taken measures necessary to maintain international peace and security.

This clearly covers Ukraine's right to fight the invader. The collective part of UN article 51 includes at least NATO article 5 type of situations and various forms of assistance to a country under attack. It is a question of ethics and political prudence as to whether aid and assistance should include military hardware, training, and intelligence. The world could do much more than it is currently doing to assist Ukraine in terms of debt forgiveness, budgetary support, and funding programmes of reconstruction, but the idea that the EU for example (and perhaps in particular) should give military support to Ukraine seems somewhat less convincing to me. Nonetheless, UN member states are legally free – unless their national laws say otherwise – to do so and there is only a thin line between the arms trade and military assistance. On the other hand, the more extensive and intensive the military assistance is, the easier it is to perceive the involved countries as direct parties to the conflict, which of course would be a step in the escalation process.

You argue that "the war's logic has not been one of mutual escalation reminiscent of the spiral model" and that "Russia has had escalation dominance the whole time". However, when I am referring to escalation in the sense of Jervis (1976), I am thinking about the long and complex process that preceded this war – the topic of our dialogue – not merely about the war itself. While there is no question about the fact that Russia has invaded Ukraine and that it has been the dominant party to the war in terms of its military resources, the spiral of escalation may continue further and draw in other countries, the West, or even the whole world. Moreover, I have difficulties in understanding "the old wisdom [...] that the conflict should first have reached some level of ripeness that has the characteristics of a 'mutually hurting stalemate'". This "ripeness" is a euphemism that hides the reality that every day of ripening causes about 1,000 casualties, psychosomatic terror and material destruction, and possibly the further economic collapse of Ukraine (the GDP of Ukraine is likely to collapse by 45% in 2022 – which in 2021 in dollar terms was less than the GDP of Finland, a country with a population of only five million). I concur with Michael Walzer (2006, 22) when he states bluntly that modern "war is hell". Finally, in light of our previous discussions, I once again wonder whether your criticism of "Westsplaining" implies that this war is a separate and isolated conflict ultimately caused by the intrinsically imperialist nature of Russia, or some such; and that therefore this conflict has few if any connections to the manifold developments since the 1990s discussed in the previous chapters; or that Ukraine is not dependent on the West and thus responsive to its messages or will (also in the Deutschian sense of "will"; see note 6 in Chapter 4).

In any event, uncertainty about the nature of the situation prevails, especially as the Russian decision to invade seems to have stemmed from a reaction to an (in part self-caused) situation at the apex of two decades of step-by-step conflict escalation. This reaction was aggravated by organisational stupidity. The point is that uncertainty raises further questions. Do we really know what Russia's war aims are? Even if the war aims of the Kremlin were well-specified at the outset of the war, do they remain well-specified now, or in the future? Do we even know whether the main actors in Moscow have a clear idea about the war aims? What they now say in public may perhaps be seen as a series of rationalisations and/or results of a long process of escalation. What the authoritarian nationalist-populists in Russia have adopted by 2022 looks like a version of the idea of a Greater Russia, which is defined in terms of ethnicity and language, but is that their firm and fixed aim or something that is negotiable? As uncertainty prevails, there must be room for concessions.

You advocate the "containment" of Russia. I agree that significant sanctions against Russia are necessary to express commitment to the basic norms of international society and the global industrial civilisation. However, it would have been wise to avoid such excessive sanctions that primarily hit the Russian or European population, have severe effects on food security for many countries in northern Africa and the Middle East, and may further escalate tensions at the risk of a direct military confrontation with Russia. On the one hand, you write that "the new Cold War is not an ideological conflict" (although I can also see a clash of world-historical narratives); on the other hand, you also write that "Russia has aimed at changing the whole world order" (whereas I would rather agree with Sakwa (2016, 30–34) and characterise Russia's aims as neo-revisionism). Leaving these kinds of tensions aside, while containment is a Cold War term, it has deeper mythological foundations. In Manichean thinking based on a dualistic cosmology exhibiting the struggle between good and evil, the latter must be contained so that light and darkness can finally be separated over time through battles. This kind of mythological absolutism is not only dangerous in the world of nuclear weapons and ecological crises, but it also disregards such complexities as:

(1) the actions of the other are always to some extent caused or produced by the self (what you do has effects on how "good" and "bad" possibilities in the other come to being; note 11 in Chapter 4; also Jervis 1976);
(2) the public affairs stemming from the interconnectedness of Russia with the rest of the world will disappear nowhere because of this war.

Attempts to punish Russia by disconnecting and containing it feed the process of dividing the world into two camps. There is a tendency that, once you establish sanctions, they will stay on for many years. Even if there is a regime change in Russia, it does not necessarily mean their abolition. From the Russian point of view, this indicates two possibilities – either import substitution or refocussing on the Asian markets. They have already been doing both since 2014 and they will be doing much more in the coming years. The same is true of attempts to exclude Russia from SWIFT (the Belgium-based Society for Worldwide Interbank Financial Telecommunication). China as well as some countries in Europe can use alternative payment channels to keep euro and renminbi payments flowing to Russia. Already in March 2022, more than half of Russian exports were *not* dollar-denominated, and this share is rapidly increasing. To make financial sanctions against Russia efficient, the US and the EU would have to display a clear willingness to also sanction Chinese and Indian banks, among others (see e.g. Greene 2022).

Attempts to disconnect and contain Russia mean that Russia will turn increasingly towards China, India, and other "friendly" countries. Simultaneously, these attempts will also contribute to the further decline of the US, for example through the position of the US dollar in the world economy. Although from the perspective of China, India, and many countries in the global south, Russia's invasion of Ukraine violates international law, this conflict resonates with other issues and conflicts in the world. The historical arrogance of the West and the enlargement of NATO are seen as part of the problem. Many recall the unilateral wars waged by the West (which we have discussed above), not least in the Middle East. Moreover, governments representing at least half of humanity believe that Russia's legitimate security interests have not been taken into account. Many actors across the world are not afraid of Russia but see that it is in their interests to cooperate with it.

The most worrying aspect of this conflict concerns nuclear weapons. Soon after the beginning of the invasion, Putin declared that they had set their nuclear deterrence to high alert. Although this may not have meant much in practice, it is concerning in light of the recently modified Russian doctrine that Russia can retaliate with nuclear weapons against an existential threat (the US doctrine is similar). In times of crisis, misperceptions and technical problems are more likely to cause a nuclear war than during more tranquil times. Arguably, the world has not been this close to a nuclear war since the Cuban crisis of 1962. As you say, the Russian leadership have now used the fear of escalation towards a nuclear war for their benefit, which has negative consequences for the nuclear non-proliferation regime. In any case, I am convinced we agree that nothing can justify the use of nuclear weapons. Yet I am concerned about the tendency to downplay or sideline the problem. As I argued above, in rational decision-making any course of action is always better than those that increase the risk of a nuclear war even slightly. The only rational course of action would be to work towards a world where the possibility of a nuclear war, whether limited or all-out, is zero.

The Ukraine War has once again brought to light the insanity of a world where some states have nuclear weapons and have concentrated this cosmic destructive power in the hands of a few leaders. If humanity learns anything from this crisis, it is that the planetary era of jets, missiles, satellites, and nuclear weapons has to come to an end without the actualisation of the destructive power of nuclear weapons – and the sooner the better. The nuclear problematic is complex (see e.g. Deudney 2006; Cronberg 2021; Pearson & Simpson 2022) and we do not have the space to discuss it in sufficient detail, but let me just make three quick points. First, the deterioration of Russia–US relations has occurred in the context of systematic and partly purposeful failures of arms control negotiations. The Anti-Ballistic Missile (ABM) Treaty was dismantled by President Bush in 2002 as part of the US neo-imperial turn, as discussed above (Chapter 3). This withdrawal – "a move vigorously condemned by the Russians as an assault on a key piece of the arms control architecture at the center of the settlement of the Cold War" (Deudney 2020, 169) – was motivated by the desire to free the US unilaterally from nuclear deterrence (a working missile defence system could blunt a retaliatory strike). The Intermediate-Range Nuclear Forces Treaty (INF) was dismantled by Trump in 2018 on the grounds of Russian non-compliance and the Chinese build-up of missiles (China was not a party to the treaty). The 2010 New START (Strategic Arms Reduction Treaty) almost shared the fate of these treaties, but at the last minute the new Biden administration agreed to extend the treaty for five years, until 2026. The descent towards a Hobbesian "anarchy" is clear also in this context, as is the active role of the US in the process of dismantling rules and agreements.

My second point concerns the non-proliferation regime. The Treaty on the Non-Proliferation of Nuclear Weapons (NPT, which entered into force in 1970) has two sides. On one side, non-nuclear-weapon states agree never to acquire nuclear weapons. On the other side, nuclear-weapon states are committed to total nuclear disarmament (NPT's article VI: "Each of the Parties to the Treaty undertakes to pursue negotiations in good faith on effective measures relating to cessation of the nuclear arms race at an early date and to nuclear disarmament, and on a treaty on general and complete disarmament"). The main focus has been on the first side of the treaty. Frustrated by the lack of progress towards complete nuclear disarmament, in 2007 a global civil society coalition started to advocate a treaty on the prohibition of nuclear weapons. Eventually, after various phases, this treaty was negotiated under the auspices of the UN. In 2017, a large number of countries adopted the Treaty on the Prohibition of Nuclear Weapons, which entered into force in January 2021 (currently c. 90 states have either ratified or signed the treaty). The US has actively opposed the treaty, including by sending a letter to the signatories. This letter from the Trump administration, obtained by news agency the Associated Press, urged the signatories to withdraw from the treaty (the story is told in many places, e.g. Lederer 2020). It is not far-fetched to see these kinds of activities as a clear violation of article VI of the NPT Treaty.

My third and final point is directly related to the war in Ukraine. Oscar Arias, Nobel Peace Prize laureate and president of Costa Rica from 1986–1990 and 2006–2010, and Jonathan Granoff, director of the Global Security Institute, have made an interesting suggestion regarding the war in Ukraine and nuclear disarmament (Arias & Granoff 2022). They propose that the US should unilaterally start to withdraw all nuclear weapons from Europe and Turkey. This would be an initiative that could bring the Kremlin to the negotiating table and possibly agree to end the war in Ukraine. This proposal would be a sign of the US effort to de-escalate the increasingly destructive war in Ukraine. This move would also deprive Putin of one of his most important arguments for Russian aggression. The global nuclear deterrence of the US and Europe's conventional defence capability would remain intact. The withdrawal of nuclear weapons would constitute an altercasting strategy on the part of the US. Equally importantly, the move could also trigger a turning point in global disarmament negotiations towards a more constructive and progressive direction.

TF: True, the risk of the war going nuclear cannot be ignored. Although the loose nuclear talk is part of Russia's tactics to frighten the West, it has lowered the threshold for their use. It is not likely that in the current situation Russia would start to use them, and the West should not give in for the sake of mere nuclear blackmailing. The key purpose is to keep the Western forces out of Ukraine. Yet, should Putin and the other Russian leaders define the denial of their victory in the war as an existential threat, many analysts fear that Russia might resort to nuclear weapons out of despair (see Sukin 2022). I do not see this as probable, but the likelihood of a nuclear war has definitely grown. Even if Russia did not use them, the chances of nuclear proliferation continuing and one state somewhere resorting to their use is worrisome, because the nuclear taboo may be eroding. Developing smaller and more precise nuclear weapons is dangerous in this regard (Tannenwald 2022). The present war should indeed lead to worldwide nuclear disarmament as the risks have become plain, but many states may draw the opposite conclusion, namely that only nuclear weapons can build a true deterrent.

I agree that NATO should rethink its nuclear strategy. However, I am sceptical as to whether a proposal for a unilateral withdrawal of US nuclear weapons from Europe would help to end the war at this stage. Tactical nuclear weapons are not crucial for deterring Russia, and European citizens do not want to have nuclear weapons on their soil, but it is Russia that has invested in such weapons more recently. As the amount of US nuclear weapons has already been radically reduced since the Cold War, some sort of reciprocity could also be expected in this matter. Trump's decision to withdraw the US from the INF Treaty was symbolic since the treaty was one of the first steps in the rapprochement between the US and the Soviet Union at the end of the Cold War but, as you say, Russia had already violated the treaty for several years.

HP: I appreciate your scepticism as a sign of critical thinking, yet it seems to me that you recognise the problem of nuclear weapons without drawing rational conclusions from it. This is likely because you assume – as we have discussed recurrently by now – that problems also in this field are by and large, if not exclusively, caused by Russia, even though it was the US that pulled out of the INF Treaty and so forth, as I explained above. Even at the risk of over-interpreting you and repeating myself, this kind of thinking may come down to simple Manicheanism whereby "our" (the US or Western) nuclear weapons are good (they "deter"), while the nuclear weapons of others are bad (they "threaten"). If both sides see the situation in equally Manichean terms, the outcome is highly unstable and dangerous. In the real world where uncertainty prevails, there are several ways in which parties may come to define the situation in a manner that could justify the first use of nuclear weapons. Moreover, it is not possible to extrapolate guidelines from the past. So far, the only time nuclear weapons have been used was in 1945, by the US against Japan. On top of all other considerations, a nuclear war can start accidentally. The decline of trust in the context of a crisis or war increases the likelihood of an accidental nuclear catastrophe. While it is true that in the current context the most acute risk lies in Russia resorting to nuclear weapons, the big picture must include long-term processes, many relevant actors, as well as various unknowns and surprises.

In my big picture analysis, as already stressed, the basic problem is that the neo-imperialist turn of the early 2000s, the global financial crisis of 2007–2008, and subsequent regressive developments including in and through Russia, have taken the world towards practices and situations that resemble those of the turn of the 19th and 20th centuries. Given the existence of jets, missiles, satellites, nuclear weapons and so on, this also means a new round of the Cold War, namely another round of "Russian roulette" for humanity. Either way, the world has returned to a stage where it is once again of utmost urgency to engage with confidence-building and arms control measures for restraining the increasingly dangerous global security dynamics. We must get back to the future. To reiterate, what we see is not merely a divided Cold War world but simultaneously also a world of complex interdependence. This interdependence defines worldwide relations of power through value chains, the overlap between different national jurisdictions, global networks of informational and financial exchange, a global formation of aggregate efficient demand, and so forth. The steps taken so far to govern this interdependence are grossly inadequate in view of countering the main contradictions and mechanisms pushing the world through various processes towards a global military catastrophe.

Over time, confidence-building and arms control measures should be followed by disarmament. Radical disarmament, in particular, can be seen as an important step in a transition towards a legitimate monopoly of means of (mass) violence at the global level, namely towards a world state (cf. Deudney 2006). However, we have known since Karl Deutsch et al. (1957) that the existence of the state is not a necessary or a sufficient condition for peace, and nor is the non-existence of the state a necessary or a sufficient condition for the prevalence of the acute threat of political violence. These connections are contingent (for a systematic discussion on the idea of world statehood, see Patomäki 2023). The imposition of anything like a common government, with its capability of violent enforcement of norms, may well decrease rather than increase the chances of peace (a unilateral attempt by one or more states to impose a global "monarchy" is even worse in this regard). The two transformations depicted in Figure 6.1 are possible both within and in the absence of a common state or hierarchical rule. In a security community, actors have come to agree on at least this one point: that conflicts over common issues (*res publica*) must and can be resolved by processes of peaceful change. This agreement is not just a matter of belief. Rather, it is a result of the gradual institutionalisation of expectations, practices, and procedures, which give real and enduring grounds for a mutual and generalised understanding that actors do not (have reasons to) prepare for the use of organised military violence, either to preserve the status quo or to foster changes.

The complex process of security community construction may not be directly linked to security or military affairs yet, if successful, integration results in desecuritisation. The building of institutions to solve common problems and overcome various contradictions of the global political economy generates integration understood in terms of dependable expectation of peaceful changes and a sense of community. Consider the case of climate change. The climate movement may eventually convince a coalition of governments to change the existing or create new international law. If actors can establish new organisations such as a democratically organised global greenhouse gas tax in response to the climate crisis, the impact of this breakthrough can be massive in different sectors of governance, from health to economy and security. This would also shape global security dynamics. Or consider another example: the separation of Russia from SWIFT and the dollar system. The sanctions are now dividing the world into two camps of competing payment systems. The dividing world starts to resemble the world of Orwell's *Nineteen Eighty-Four* where there is a constant state of war between Oceania, Eurasia, and East Asia. Instead of such disintegration, we need global integration and a worldwide clearing union that is based on cosmopolitan equality and legality (Kotilainen 2022).

A final word on equality and struggles over its recognition. Earlier in our dialogue, you mentioned that the "West tried to avoid humiliating Russia by treating it as a great power, but it did not regard Russia as a superpower equal to the US". In turn, I referred to the contrast between the OSCE, in which Russia has been recognised as an equal member, and NATO, where the US is positioned as the leader. These struggles revolve around the recognition of equality among particular kinds of states, namely "great powers". In the US–Russia context, both parties seem to take as given the fundamental inequality between great powers and other states. The US stand can be read as implying that there is one superpower and a few somewhat lesser great powers (perhaps the other veto powers of the UN Security Council); whereas Russia insists that it must be recognised as a fully equal member of the club of great powers. From the point of view of global integration, peaceful changes, and a sense of the world or planetary community, these struggles over hierarchy and recognition are not only hopelessly anachronistic but also counterproductive, if the aim is to strengthen common rules and the conditions for peace. To get back to the future, we need much more democratic ways of understanding what the recognition of equality means, ultimately pointing towards world citizenship and global democracy.

TF: Perhaps we should, indeed, end our dialogue with some more optimistic visions, although there is no certainty of any progress in history. However, we might be able to see the war not as the first full-scale war of the 21st century in Europe, but rather as the last of the 20th century. If we tend to agree that this war could have been avoided, we could hope that it will provide lessons that are solid enough for avoiding future wars of similar scale. There is no need to revise all theories and judgments that give us hope. The optimistic liberal theory has been wrong in some of its assumptions. For example, the idea of interdependence created by trade relations being a factor preventing war has lost much of its plausibility because of the Ukrainian War, but the general perspective of progress and decline of violence has not been discredited (e.g. Pinker 2011; Inglehart et al. 2015). The global triumph of democracy has not materialised, but the dystopic vision of a global turn towards autocracy is not a univocal trend either, despite all the challenges of authoritarian populism, societal polarisation, and manipulative algorithms that the established democracies are now facing (see e.g. IDEA 2021). International mechanisms of global governance are anything but perfect, but they are much more robust than they were during the previous centuries. I agree that the idea of great powers and their persistent rivalry should be overcome by making the hierarchies more flexible and less dependent on military power. The idea of global democracy should be strengthened. The biggest task is in any case related to global ecological problems and sustainability that require the full concentration of all states and nations. Of course, we cannot ignore the massive risks and challenges that the war in Ukraine may accelerate and pose not only to our Western societies but to the whole world. However, if the collective optimism that was allegedly taken for granted turned out to be a failure in the 1990s, a collective pessimism about the future in 2022 would be equally problematic.

Notes

1 If the analogy to the Winter War in 1939–1940 between the Soviet Union and Finland is applied, the Ukraine War does not wholly resemble it. In the Winter War, Russia's invasion was halted for a while at first, and then its military superiority by sheer numbers became apparent. Despite this, Finnish public opinion was not willing to accept a peace deal that comprised major losses of territory, even areas that the Soviet Union had not militarily occupied. The interim peace was not durable, but territorial losses were duly accepted after a renewed lost war in 1941–1944. The peace deal ending the Winter War was possible partly because Stalin feared Western intervention in the war if it was prolonged, and the Finnish leaders started to believe that Nazi Germany was not going to give the Soviet Union a free hand with regard to Finland, and that they might even get the lost territories back if

Nazi Germany attacked the Soviet Union. Moreover, the war had mainly been a front war without too many civilian casualties or atrocities committed.

2 In addition to Henry Kissinger and Noam Chomsky (see Stanton 2022), who have advocated that Ukraine should accept territorial losses for peace, Jeffrey Sachs (2022), for example, has opined that "practically speaking, to save Ukraine, we need to end the war, and to end the war, we need a compromise, in which Russia goes home and NATO does not enlarge". However, such a peace plan seems to be completely out of touch with Russia's current war aims. See also the Open Letter by German Intellectuals titled "A Ceasefire Now!" published in *Die Zeit* Online on 29 June 2022, and Umland et al. (2022) for a reply from almost a hundred Eastern European and Russian Studies scholars to that open letter. Umland et al. also make the point that very few or hardly any of these "German intellectuals" had any background in studying Russia or Ukraine.

Bibliography

Agrawal, Ravi (2022). "Former NATO Chief: we 'overestimated' Russia's military: Anders Fogh Rasmussen speaks to FP about Russian President Vladimir Putin's war in Ukraine, the future of NATO, and more". *Foreign Policy Online*, available at https://foreignpolicy.com/2022/06/06/russia-nato-war-anders-fogh-rasmussen-ukraine/.

Allan, Duncan and Wolczuk, Kataryna (2022). "Why Minsk-2 Cannot Solve the Ukraine Crisis". *Chatham House Explainer*, 16 February 2022, available at www.chathamhouse.org/2022/02/why-minsk-2-cannot-solve-ukraine-crisis, accessed 17 March 2022.

Allen, Robert C. (2001). "The Rise and Decline of the Soviet Economy". *The Canadian Journal of Economics / Revue canadienne d'Economique*, 34:4, 859–881.

Ambrosio, Thomas (2005). "The Russo-American Dispute Over the Invasion of Iraq: international status and the role of positional goods". *Europe-Asia Studies*, 57:8, 1189–1210.

Angell, Norman (1909). *The Great Illusion. A Study of the Relation of Military Power to National Advantage.* 4th enlarged edition. New York & London: G.P. Putnam's Sons.

Arendt, Hannah (1958). *The Human Condition.* Chicago: The University of Chicago Press.

Arias, Oscar and Granoff, Jonathan (2022). "Nuclear Strategy and Ending the War in Ukraine". *The Hill*, 19 July 2022, available at https://thehill.com/opinion/international%20/3565996-nuclear-strategy-and-ending-the-war-in-ukraine/.

Åtland, Kristian (2020). "Destined for Deadlock? Russia, Ukraine, and the unfulfilled Minsk agreements". *Post-Soviet Affairs*, 36:2, 122–139.

Belton, Catherine (2020). *Putin's People: How the KGB Took Back Russia and Then Took on the West.* London: William Collins.

Berger, Thomas and Luckmann, Peter L. (1991 [1966]) *The Social Construction of Reality: A Treatise in the Sociology of Knowledge.* London: Penguin.

Bhaskar, Roy (1979). *The Possibility of Naturalism.* Brighton: The Harvester Press.

Bhaskar, Roy (1986). *Scientific Realism and Human Emancipation*. London: Verso.
Blum, William (2002). *Rogue State. A Guide to the World's Only Superpower*. Revised 2nd edition. London & New York: Zed Books.
Bouchet, Nicolas (2016). "Russia's 'Militarization' of Colour Revolutions: since Ukraine's EuroMaidan, Russia sees mass anti-regime protests at home and abroad as a military threat". *CSS Policy Perspectives*, 4:2, available at www.css.ethz.ch/content/dam/ethz/special-interest/gess/cis/center-for-securities-studies/pdfs/PP4-2.pdf.
Bremmer, Ian and Charap, Samuel (2007). "The Siloviki in Putin's Russia: who they are and what they want". *The Washington Quarterly*, 30:1, 83–92.
Brzezinski, Zbigniew (1997). *The Grand Chessboard: American Primacy and its Geostrategic Imperatives*. New York: Basic Books.
Burns, William (2019). *The Back Channel*. London: C. Hurst & Co. Publishers.
Cafruny, Alan, Fouskas, Vassilis, Mallinson, William and Voynitsky, Andrey (2022). "Ukraine, Multipolarity and the Crisis of Grand Strategies". *Journal of Balkan and Near Eastern Studies*, an early view version available at DOI: 10.1080/19448953.2022.2084881
Chayes, Abram, Olson, Lara and Raach, George (1997). "The Development of U.S. Policy Toward the Former Soviet Union" in Arbatov, Alexei, Chayes, Abram, Handler Chayes, Antonia, and Olson, Lara (eds), Managing Conflict in the Former Soviet Union: Russian and American Perspectives, 493–536. Cambridge: The MIT Press.
Chowdhury, Anwarul (2022). "Veto is the Chief Culprit but Expulsion or Suspension Is Not the Remedy". *Internet Press Service News Agency*, 8 March 2022, available at www.ipsnews.net/2022/03/veto-chief-culprit-expulsion-suspension-not-remedy/, accessed 17 March 2022.
Clark, Christopher (2013). *The Sleepwalkers: How Europe Went to War in 1914*. New York: HarperCollins.
Coalson, Robert (2014). "Putin Pledges To protect All Ethnic Russians Anywhere. So, Where Are They?". *Radio Free Europe/Radio Liberty*, 10 April 2014, available at www.rferl.org/a/russia-ethnic-russification-baltics-kazakhstan-soviet/25328281.html, accessed 25 October 2022.
Conradi, Peter (2017). *Who Lost Russia? How the World Entered a New Cold War*. London: Oneworld.
Cronberg, Tarja (2021) *Renegotiating the Nuclear Order: A Sociological Approach*. Abingdon and New York: Routledge.
Dalsjö, Robert, Jonsson, Michael and Norberg, Johan (2022). "A Brutal Examination: Russian Military Capability in Light of the Ukraine War". *Survival*, 64:3, 7–28.
Delcour, Laure and Wolczuk, Kataryna (2015). "Spoiler or Facilitator of Democratization? Russia's Role in Georgia and Ukraine". *Democratization*, 22:3, 459–478.
Derbyshire, James and Morgan, Jamie (2022) "Is Seeking Certainty in Climate Sensitivity Measures Counterproductive in the Context of Climate Emergency? The case for scenario planning". *Technological*

Bibliography

Forecasting & Social Change, 182, 1–11, DOI: https://doi.org/10.1016/j.techfore.2022.121811

Deudney, Daniel (2006). *Bounding Power: Republican Security Theory from the Polis to the Global Village*. Princeton, NJ: Princeton University Press.

Deudney, Daniel (2020). *Dark Skies: Space Expansionism, Planetary Geopolitics, and the Ends of Humanity*. New York: Oxford University Press.

Deudney, Daniel and Ikenberry, G. John (2021). "Seeds of Failure: the end of the Cold War and the failure of the Russian democratic transition and Western integration". In Monteiro, Nuno P. and Bartel, Fritz (eds), *Before and After the Fall: World Politics and the End of the Cold War*. Cambridge: Cambridge University Press.

Deutsch, Karl W., Sidney A. Burrell, Robert A. Kann, Maurice Lee Jr., Martin Lichterman, Raymond E. Lindgren, Francis L. Loewenheim, and Richard W. van Wagenen (1957). *Political Community and the North Atlantic Area. International Organization in the Light of Historical Experience*. Princeton, NJ: Princeton University Press.

Deutsch, Karl (1963). *The Nerves of Government. Models of Political Communication and Control*. New York: The Free Press.

Deutsche Welle (2008). "Russia Talks Tough in Response to NATO's Eastward Expansion". *Deutsche Welle*, 11 April 2008, available at www.dw.com/en/russia-talks-tough-in-response-to-natos-eastward-expansion/a-3261078, accessed 16 March 2022.

Dijkstra, Hylke, Cavelty, Myriam Dunn, Jenne, Nicole and Reykers, Yf (2022). "War in Ukraine". *Contemporary Security Policy*, 43:3, 464–465.

Duncan, Peter (2013). "Russia, the West and the 2007–2008 Electoral Cycle: did the Kremlin really fear a 'coloured revolution'?". *Europe-Asia Studies*, 65:1, 1–25.

Dyson, Stephen Benedict and Parent, Matthew (2018). "The Operational Code Approach to Profiling Political Leaders: understanding Vladimir Putin". *Intelligence and National Security*, 33:1, 84–100.

Edmunds, Lowell (1975). *Chance and Intelligence in Thucydides*. Harvard: Harvard University Press.

EU (2017). "Shared Vision, Common Action: a Stronger Europe. A global strategy for the European Union's foreign and security policy". *Publications Office of the European Union*, available at https://data.europa.eu/doi/10.2871/9875, accessed 7 July 2022.

Farrell, Henry and Newman, Abraham L. (2019). "Weaponized Interdependence: how global economic networks shape state coercion". *International Security*, 44:1, 42–79.

Forsberg, Tuomas (1995). "Territorial Disputes and the Possibility of Peaceful Change". In Patomäki, Heikki (ed.), *Peaceful Changes in World Politics*, 122–167. Tampere: Tampere Peace Research Institute.

Forsberg, Tuomas (2002). *Nato-kirja [The NATO Book]*. Ajatus: Helsinki.

Forsberg, Tuomas (2019). "Explaining Russian Foreign Policy towards the EU through Contrasts". *International Politics*, 56:6, 762–777.

Forsberg, Tuomas and Haukkala, Hiski (2016). *The European Union and Russia*. London: Palgrave Macmillan.

Forsberg, Tuomas and Herd, Graeme (2015). "Russia and NATO: from windows of opportunities to closed doors". *Journal of Contemporary European Studies*, 23:1, 41–57.

Forsberg, Tuomas and Pesu, Matti (2016). "The 'Finlandization' of Finland: the ideal type, the historical model, and the lessons learned". *Diplomacy and Statecraft*, 27:3, 473–495.

Forsberg, Tuomas and Pursiainen, Christer (2017). "The Psychological Dimension of Russian Foreign Policy: Putin and the annexation of Crimea". *Global Society*, 31:2, 220–244.

Galtung, Johan (2002). "September 11 2001: diagnosis, prognosis, therapy". In Galtung, J. Jacobsen, C.G. and Brand-Jacobsen, K. (eds), *Searching for Peace: The Road to TRANSCEND*, 87–102. London: Pluto Press.

Garfinkel, Alan (1981). *Forms of Explanation: Rethinking the Questions in Social Theory*. New Haven: Yale University Press.

Gelman, Vladimir (2015). *Authoritarian Russia: Analyzing Post-Soviet Regime Changes*. Pittsburgh: University of Pittsburgh Press.

Gerstle, Gary (2022). *The Rise and Fall of the Neoliberal Order. America and the World in the Free Market Era*. Oxford: Oxford University Press.

Giddens, Anthony (1981). *A Contemporary Critique of Historical Materialism*, vol. 1. Berkeley: University of California Press.

Goldgeier, Jim (2019). "Promises Made, Promises Broken? What Yeltsin was told about NATO in 1993 and why it matters". *War on the Rocks*, 22 November 2019, available at https://warontherocks.com/2019/11/promises-made-promises-broken-what-yeltsin-was-told-about-nato-in-1993-and-why-it-matters-2/.

Goodman, Amy (2022). "The West's False Narrative about Russia and China". Interview of Jeffrey D. Sachs. *Democracy Now!* 30 August 2022, available at www.jeffsachs.org/newspaper-articles/h29g9k7l7fymxp39yhzwxc5f72ancr.

Gorin, Zeev (1985). "Socialist Societies and World System Theory: a critical survey". *Science & Society*, 49:3, 332–366.

Greene, Robert (2022). "How Sanctions on Russia Will Alter Global Payments Flows". *Carnegie Endowment for Peace*, 4 March 2022, available at https://carnegieendowment.org/2022/03/04/how-sanctions-on-russia-will-alter-global-payments-flows-pub-86575.

Griffiths, Rudyart (ed.) (2015). *Should the West Engage Putin's Russia? Pozner and Cohen vs. Applebaum and Kasparov. The Munk Debates*. Toronto: Anansi.

Hardt, Michael and Negri, Antonio (2000) *Empire*. Cambridge, MA: Harvard University Press.

Harris, Shane, DeYoung, Karen, Khurshudyan, Isabelle, Parker, Ashley and Sly, Liz (2022). "Road to War: U.S. struggled to convince allies, and Zelensky, of risk of invasion". *The Washington Post*, 16 August 2022, available at www.washingtonpost.com/national-security/interactive/2022/ukraine-road-to-war/?itid=sf_world_ukraine-russia_more-coverage-2, accessed 17 August 2022.

Harvey, David (2005). *A Brief History of Neoliberalism*. Oxford: Oxford University Press.
Harvey, Frank (2013). *Explaining the Iraq War: Counterfactual Theory, Logic and Evidence*. Cambridge: Cambridge University Press.
Herwig, Holger (2006). "Hitler Wins in the East but Germany Still Loses World War II". In Tetlock, Philip, Lebow, Richard Ned and Parker, Geoffrey (eds), *Unmaking the West. "What-if?" Scenarios that Rewrite World History*, 323–360. Ann Arbor: The University of Michigan Press.
Hill, William (2018). *No Place for Russia: European Security Institutions Since 1989*. New York: Columbia University Press.
Hill, William (2021). "Putin on Moldova: what can we still learn from a 2003 failure?" *The Russia File*, 15 January 2021, available at www.wilsoncenter.org/blog-post/putin-moldova-what-can-we-still-learn-2003-failure, accessed 10 August 2022.
Hoffman, David (2000). "Putin Says 'Why Not?' to Russia Joining NATO". *The Washington Post*, 6 March 2000, available at www.washingtonpost.com/archive/politics/2000/03/06/putin-says-why-not-to-russia-joining-nato/c1973032-c10f-4bff-9174-8cae673790cd/.
Hopf, Ted (2016). "'Crimea is Ours': a discursive history". *International Relations*, 30:2, 227–255.
Horovitz, Liviu (2021) "A 'Great Prize,' But Not the Main Prize: British internal deliberations on not-losing Russia, 1993–1995". In Schmies, Oxana (ed.), *NATO's Enlargement and Russia: A Strategic Challenge in the Past and Future*, 85–112. Stuttgart: ididem.
IDEA (2021) *Global State of Democracy Report 2021: Building Resilience in a Pandemic Era*. Stockholm: International IDEA.
Inglehart, Ronald, Puranen, Bi and Welzel, Christian (2015). "Declining Willingness to Fight for One's Country: the individual-level basis of the long peace". *Journal of Peace Research*, 52:4, 418–434.
Jervis, Robert (1976). *Perception and Misperception in International Politics*. Princeton, NJ: Princeton University Press.
Keal, Paul (1983). "Contemporary Understanding About Spheres of Influence". *Review of International Studies*, 9:3, 155–172.
Kennan, George ["X"] (1947). "The Sources of Soviet Conduct". *Foreign Affairs*, 25:3, 566–582.
Khaldarova, I. (2021). "Brother or 'Other'? Transformation of strategic narratives in Russian television news during the Ukrainian crisis". *Media, War and Conflict*, 14:1, 3–20.
Klußmann, Uwe, Schepp, Matthias and Wiegrefe, Klaus (2009). "Did the West Break Its Promise to Moscow?". *Der Spiegel International*, 26 November 2009, available at www.spiegel.de/international/world/nato-s-eastward-expansion-did-the-West-break-its-promise-to-moscow-a-663315.html, accessed 16 March 2022.
Koskenniemi, Martti (2005). *From Apology to Utopia. The Structure of International Legal Argument*. Reissue with new epilogue. Cambridge: Cambridge University Press.

Kotilainen, Konsta (2022). "Towards an International Clearing Union (At Last)? Normative underpinnings and elements of institutional design". Helsinki Centre for Global Political Economy Working Paper, 06/2022. Helsinki: University of Helsinki, available at www2.helsinki.fi/en/networks/global-political-economy/working-paper-62022.
Kotilainen, Konsta and Patomäki, Heikki (2022). "From Fragmentation to Integration: on the role of explicit hypotheses and economic theory in Global Political Economy". *Global Political Economy*, 1:1, 80–107.
Kramer, Mark (2009). "The Myth of a No-NATO-Enlargement Pledge to Russia". *The Washington Quarterly*, 32:2, 39–61.
Krause, Joachim (2019). "How Do Wars End? A strategic perspective". *Journal of Strategic Studies*, 42:7, 920–945, DOI: 10.1080/01402390.2019.1615460
Kuzio, Taras (2017). *Putin's War Against Ukraine: Revolution, Nationalism, and Crime*. Toronto: Chair of Ukrainian Studies, University of Toronto.
Laaneots, Ants (2016). "The Russian–Georgian War of 2008: causes and implication". Transl. by K. Salum. *Endc Occasional Papers* 4/2016. Tartu: Estonian National Defence College.
Lawson, Tony (2022). "Social Positioning Theory and Quantum Mechanics". Mimeo, draft, 18 July 2022. Cambridge: University of Cambridge.
Lebow, Richard Ned (2010a). *Forbidden Fruit*. Counterfactuals and International Relations. Princeton, NJ: Princeton University Press.
Lebow, Richard Ned (2010b). *Why Nations Fight: Past and Future Motives for War*. Cambridge: Cambridge University Press.
Lebow, Richard Ned (2014). *Archduke Franz Ferdinand Lives! A World Without World War I*. New York: Palgrave Macmillan.
Lederer, Edith (2020). "US Urges Countries to Withdraw from UN Nuclear Ban Treaty". *The Times of Israel*, 22 October 2020, available at www.timesofisrael.com/us-urges-countries-to-withdraw-from-un-nuclear-ban-treaty/.
Lester, Jeremy (1994). "Russian Political Attitudes to Ukrainian Independence". *The Journal of Communist Studies and Transition Politics*, 10:2, 193–233.
Levy, Jack (2015). "Counterfactuals, Causal Inference, and Historical Analysis". *Security Studies*, 24:3, 378–402.
Levy, Jack and Vasquez, John (eds) (2014). *The Outbreak of the First World War: Structure, Politics and Decision-Making*. Cambridge: Cambridge University Press.
Mälksoo, Maria (2022). "The Postcolonial Moment in Russia's War Against Ukraine". *Journal of Genocide Research*, DOI: 10.1080/14623528.2022.2074947
Mareeva, Svetlana (2020). "Socio-Economic Inequalities in Modern Russia and Their Perception by the Population". *Journal of Chinese Sociology*, 7:10, doi:10.1186/s40711-020-00124-9
Marten, Kimberly (2017). "Reconsidering NATO Expansion: a counterfactual analysis of Russia and the West in the 1990s". *European Journal of International Security*, 3:2, 135–161.

Mazat, Numa (2016). "Structural Analysis of the Economic Decline and Collapse of the Soviet Union". Anais do XLIII Encontro Nacional de Economia [Proceedings of the 43rd Brazilian Economics Meeting] 029, ANPEC, available at https://ideas.repec.org/p/anp/en2015/029.html.

McFaul, Michael (2018). *From Cold War to Hot Peace: An American Ambassador in Putin's Russia.* Boston, MA: Houghton Mifflin Harcourt.

Mearsheimer, John (1993). "The Case for a Ukrainian Nuclear Deterrent". *Foreign Affairs*, 72:3, 50–66.

Mearsheimer, John (2001). *The Tragedy of Great Power Politics.* New York: W.W. Norton.

Mearsheimer, John (2015). "Why is Ukraine the West's fault? Featuring John Mearsheimer". The University of Chicago, 25 September 2015, available at www.youtube.com/watch?v=JrMiSQAGOS4, accessed 16 March 2022.

Mearsheimer, John (2018). *The Great Delusion: Liberal Dreams and International Realities.* New Haven, CT: Yale University Press.

Mearsheimer, John (2022). "The Causes and Consequences of the Ukraine Crisis". *National Interest*, 22 June 2022, available at https://nationalinterest.org/feature/causes-and-consequences-ukraine-crisis-203182, accessed 27 June 2022.

Meister, Stefan (2022). "Elements of Containing Russia", *Internationale Politik Quarterly,* 29 September 2022, available at https://ip-quarterly.com/en/elements-containing-russia, accessed 30 September 2022.

Michailova, Snejina (2022). "An Attempt to Understand the War in Ukraine – an Escalation of Commitment Perspective". *British Journal of Management*, an early view version available at DOI: 10.1111/1467-8551.12633

Monthly Review (2022). "The U.S. Uses Double Standards in International Affairs: Sanders", *MRonline*, 10 March 2022, available at https://mronline.org/2022/03/10/the-u-s-uses-double-standards-in-international-affairs-sanders/, accessed 16 March 2022.

Morgan, Jamie and Patomäki, Heikki (2017). "Contrast Explanation in Economics: its context, meaning, and potential". *Cambridge Journal of Economics*, 41:5, 1391–1418.

Moshes, Arkady and Nizhnikau, Ryhor (2022). "Zelenskyy's Change of Approach Towards Russia: from soft touch to firm hand". *FIIA Briefing Paper*, 340, 31 May 2022, available at www.fiia.fi/julkaisu/zelenskyys-change-of-approach-towards-russia?read, accesssed 26 July 2022.

Moscow Times (2022). "Russian Church Leader Appears to Blame Gay Pride Parades for Ukraine War", *The Moscow Times*, 7 March 2022, available at www.themoscowtimes.com/2022/03/07/russian-church-leader-appears-to-blame-gay-pride-parades-for-ukraine-war-a76803, accessed 26 July 2022.

National Security Archive (2021). "NATO Expansion – The Budapest Blow Up 1994". *NSA*, 24 November 2021, available at https://nsarchive.gwu.edu/briefing-book/russia-programs/2021-11-24/nato-expansion-budapest-blow-1994.

Neumann, Iver B. and Pouliot, Vincent (2011) "Untimely Russia: hysteresis in Russian–Western relations over the past millennium". *Security Studies*, 20:1, 105–137.

Nyyssönen, Heino and Humphreys, Brendan (2016). "'Another Munich We Cannot Afford': historical metonymy in politics". *Redescriptions*, 19:2, 173–190.

Oltermann, Philip (2022). "Don't Compare Ukraine Invasion to First World War, Says 'Sleepwalkers' Historian". *The Guardian*, 26 June 2022, available at www.theguardian.com/world/2022/jun/26/historian-says-dont-compare-ukraine-invasion-with-his-book-on-first-world-war, accessed 7 July 2022.

O'Rourke, Lindsay and Shifrinson, Joshua (2022). "Squaring the Circle on Spheres of Influence: the overlooked benefits". *The Washington Quarterly*, 45:2, 105–124.

Pankow, T. and Patman, R.G. (2018). "Rethinking Russia's Ukraine Involvement 2013–2016: the domestic political imperatives of Putin's operational code 2018". *International Politics*, 55:5, 537–556.

Patomäki, Heikki (1995). "Hegelistä vielä kerran: onko vapautumisen dialektiikalla tulevaisuutta suvereenien valtioiden jälkeen?" [Once more on Hegel: any future for the dialectics of emancipation after the era of sovereign nation-states?]. *Kosmopolis*, 25:4, 75–83.

Patomäki, Heikki (1996). *Vain kauppakumppaneita? EU, Venäjä ja EU:n ulkosuhteiden rakenteistuminen* [*Only Trading Partners? EU, Russia and the Structuration of the External Relations of the EU*]. Helsinki: Ulkopoliittinen instituutti (Haasteita 11).

Patomäki, Heikki (ed.) (2000). *Politics of Civil Society: A Global Perspective on Democratization*. Helsinki and Nottingham: NIGD Working Paper no:2.

Patomäki, Heikki (2001). "The Challenge of Critical Theories: peace research at the start of the new century". *Journal of Peace Research*, 38:6, 723–737.

Patomäki, Heikki (2002). *After International Relations. Critical Realism and the (Re)Construction of World Politics*. London and New York: Routledge.

Patomäki, Heikki (2003). "Kohti imperiaalista maailmanjärjestystä? Analyysi sotilasliitto Naton arvoista ja sen roolista globaalissa poliittisessa taloudessa" [Towards an imperial order? An analysis of the values of NATO and its role in global political economy]. In Kangaspuro, M. and Matinpuro, T. (eds), *Uusi Nato. Eurooppalaisia näkökulmia sotilasliitosta ja Suomesta*, 11–58, Helsinki: Like.

Patomäki, Heikki (2006). "Realist Ontology for Futures Studies". *Journal of Critical Realism*, 5:1, 1–31.

Patomäki, Heikki (2008). *The Political Economy of Global Security. War, Future Crises and Changes in Global Governance*. London and New York: Routledge.

Patomäki, Heikki (2017). "Praxis, Politics and the Future: a dialectical critical realist account of world-historical causation". *Journal of International Relations and Development*, 20:4, 805–825.

Patomäki, Heikki (2018). *Disintegrative Tendencies in Global Political Economy. Exits and Conflicts*. London and New York: Routledge.

Patomäki, Heikki (2021). "Neoliberalism and Nationalist-Authoritarian Populism: explaining their constitutive and causal connections". *Protosociology. An International Journal of Interdisciplinary Research*, 37, 101–151.

Bibliography

Patomäki, Heikki (2022a). *The Three Fields of Global Political Economy*. London and New York: Routledge.
Patomäki, Heikki (2022b). "Non-Alignment of Ukraine and the No-Harm Principle of John Stuart Mill". *Brave New Europe*, 25 April 2022, available at https://braveneweurope.com/heikki-patomaki-non-alignment-of-ukraine-and-the-no-harm-principle-of-john-stuart-mill.
Patomäki, Heikki (2023) World Statehood. The Future of World Politics. Cham: Springer.
Patomäki, Heikki and Pursiainen, Christer (1998). *Against the State, With(in) the State or a Transnational Creation: Russian Civil Society in the Making*. Helsinki: Finnish Institute for International Affairs (UPI Working Papers 4/1998).
Patomäki, Heikki and Pursiainen, Christer (1999) "Western Models and the Russian Idea: beyond inside/outside in the discourses on civil society". *Millennium: Journal of International Studies*, 28:1, 53–77.
Patomäki, Heikki and Pursiainen, Christer (2004). "The State and Society in Contemporary Russian Thought". In Rindzeviciute, E. (ed.), *Contemporary Change in Russia: In from the Margins?*, 55–93. Huddinge: Beegs (Baltic & East European Studies no:3).
Pearson, Frederic and Simpson, Erika (2022). "How to De-Escalate Dangerous Nuclear Weapons and Force Deployments in Europe". *International Journal: Canada's Journal of Global Policy Analysis*, online first available at DOI: https://doi.org/10.1177/00207020221100712
Pearson, Lionel (1952). "*Prophasis* and *Aitia*". *Transactions and Proceedings of the American Philological Association*, 83, 205–223.
Pearson, Lionel (1972) "A Clarification". *Transactions and Proceedings of the American Philological Association*, 103, 381–394.
Person, Robert and McFaul, Michael (2022). "What Putin Fears Most". *Journal of Democracy* blog, 22. February 2022, available at www.journalofdemocracy.org/what-putin-fears-most/, accessed 17 March 2022.
Piccolo-Koskimies, Emanuela (2021). *Norm Contestation, Sovereignty and (Ir)Responsibility at the International Criminal Court. Debunking Liberal Anti-Politics*. Cham: Springer.
Pinker, Stephen (2011). *The Decline of Violence: The Better Angels of Our Nature*. New York: Viking.
Pohl, Rüdiger (2004). "Hindsight Bias". In Pohl, Rüdiger (ed.), *Cognitive Illusions: A Handbook on Fallacies and Biases in Thinking, Judgement and Memory*, 363–378. Hove and New York: Psychology Press
Pursiainen, Christer and Forsberg, Tuomas (2021). *The Psychology of Foreign Policy*. Cham: Palgrave Macmillan.
Putin, Vladimir (2015). "Vladimir Putin Meets with Members of the Valdai Discussion Club. Transcript of the Final Plenary Session of the 12th Annual Meeting". *Valdai Discussion Club*, 23 October 2015, available at https://valdaiclub.com/events/posts/articles/vladimir-putin-meets-with-members-of-the-valdai-discussion-club-transcript-of-the-final-plenary-sess/?sphrase_id=1374842, accessed 23 March 2022.

Putin, Vladimir (2021). "On the Historical Unity of Russians and Ukrainians". *President of Russia*, 12 July 2021, available at http://en.kremlin.ru/events/president/news/66181, accessed 16 March 2022.

Putin, Vladimir (2022). "Address by the President of the Russian Federation". *President of Russia*, 24 February 2022, available at http://en.kremlin.ru/events/president/news/67843, accessed 16 March 2022.

Rauch, Jonathan (2001). "Putin Is Right: Russia belongs in NATO". *The Atlantic*, 1 August 2001, available at www.theatlantic.com/politics/archive/2001/08/putin-is-right-russia-belongs-in-nato/377557/.

Risen, James (2022). "U.S. Intelligence Says Putin Made a Last-Minute Decision to Invade Ukraine", *The Intercept*, 11 March 2022, available at https://theintercept.com/2022/03/11/russia-putin-ukraine-invasion-us-intelligence/, accessed 26 July 2022.

Rutland, Peter (2013). "Neoliberalism and the Russian transition". *Review of International Political Economy*, 20:2, 332–362.

Sachs, Jeffrey (2022). "On Ukraine, Joe Biden Doesn't Want to Compromise". Interview by Federico Fubini. *Corriere Della Sera*, 1 May 2022, available at www.corriere.it/politica/22_maggio_01/sachs-joe-biden-doesn-t-want-to-compromise-67c95d0a-c8a1-11ec-85c4-7c8d22958d02.shtml, accessed 26 July 2022.

Sakwa, Richard (2016). *Frontline Ukraine: Crisis in the Borderlands*. London: I.B. Tauris.

Sarotte, Mary (2021). *Not One Inch: America, Russia, and the Making of Post-Cold War Stalemate*. New Haven: Yale University Press.

Sayer, Andrew (2011). *Why Things Matter to People. Social Science, Values and Ethical Life*. Cambridge: Cambridge University Press.

Sergounin, Alexander (1997). "Russian Domestic Debate on NATO Enlargement: from phobia to damage limitation". *European Security*, 6:4, 55–71.

Shifrison, Joshua (2016). "Deal or No Deal? The end of the Cold War and the U.S. offer to limit NATO expansion". *International Security*, 40:4, 7–44.

Stanton, Andrew (2022). "Henry Kissinger, Noam Chomsky Find Rare Common Ground Over Ukraine War". *Newsweek*, 24 May 2022, available at www.newsweek.com/henry-kissinger-noam-chomsky-find-rare-common-ground-over-ukraine-war-1709733.

Statista (2022). "Oil and Gas Revenue to the Federal Budget in Russia from 2006 to 2021". *Statista*, 25 February 2022, available at www.statista.com/statistics/1028682/russia-federal-budget-oil-and-gas-revenue/, accessed 16 March 2022.

Stiglitz, Joseph (2003). "The Ruin of Russia". *The Guardian*, 9 April 2003, available at www.theguardian.com/world/2003/apr/09/russia.artsandhumanities, accessed 17 March 2022.

Stoner, Kathryn (2021). *Russia Resurrected: Its Power and Purpose in a New Global Order*. Oxford: Oxford University Press.

Sukin, Laura (2022). "Has the Russia–Ukraine War Blown up the Global Nuclear Order?" *Bulletin of the Atomic Scientists*, 28 June 2022, available at https://thebulletin.org/2022/06/has-the-russia-ukraine-war-blown-up-the-global-nuclear-order/, accessed 27 July 2022.

Bibliography

Sussex, Matthew (2022). "Are Vladimir Putin's Nuclear Threats a Bluff? In a word – probably". *The Conversation*, 28 July 2022, available at https://theconversation.com/are-vladimir-putins-nuclear-threats-a-bluff-in-a-word-probably-187689.

Tannenwald, Nina (2022). "'Limited' Tactical Nuclear Weapons Would Be Catastrophic". *Scientific American*, 10 March 2022, available at www.scientificamerican.com/article/limited-tactical-nuclear-weapons-would-be-catastrophic/, accessed 10 August 2022.

Taskinen, Mika-Matti (2021):"Venäjän utopististen vaatimusten lista kasvatti sodan todennäköisyyttä Ukrainassa, arvioi professori" [Russia's utopian list of demands increased the likelihood of war]. *Suomenmaa*, 18 December 2021, available at www.suomenmaa.fi/uutiset/venajan-utopististen-vaatimusten-lista-kasvatti-sodan-todennakoisyytta-ukrainassa-arvioi-professori-2/, accessed 17 March 2022.

Tetlock, Philip (1999). "Theory-Driven Reasoning About Plausible Pasts and Probable Futures in World Politics: are we prisoners of our preconceptions?". *American Journal of Political Science*, 43:2, 335–366.

Tetlock, Philip (2005) *Expert Political Judgment. How Good Is It? How Can We Know?* Princeton, NJ: Princeton University Press.

Tetlock, Philip, Lebow, Richard Ned and Parker, Geoffrey (eds) (2006). *Unmaking the West. "What-if?" Scenarios that Rewrite World History*. Ann Arbor: The University of Michigan Press.

Tetlock, Philip and Visser, Pennyt (2000). "Thinking about Russia: plausible pasts and probable futures". *British Journal of Social Psychology*, 39(2), 173–196.

Tharoor, Ishaan (2022). "Putin Makes His Imperial Pretensions Clear". *The Washington Post*, 13 June 2022, available at www.washingtonpost.com/world/2022/06/13/putin-imperial-russia-empire-ukraine/, accessed 26 July 2022.

Trevelyan, Mark (2022). "Putin Says No One Can Win a Nuclear War". *Reuters*, 1 August 2022, available at www.reuters.com/world/putin-there-can-be-no-winners-nuclear-war-it-should-never-be-started-2022-08-01/, accessed 16 August 2022.

Thucydides (1972 [1954]). *The Peloponnesian War*. Trans. by R. Warner. London: Penguin Books. [The original text c. 400 BC.]

Traynor, Ian (2014). "Putin Claims Russian Forces 'Could Conquer Ukraine Capital in Two Weeks". *The Guardian*, 2 September 2014, available at www.theguardian.com/world/2014/sep/02/putin-russian-forces-could-conquer-ukraine-capital-kiev-fortnight, accessed 15 August 2022.

Tsygankov, Andrei (2018). "The Sources of Russia's Fear of NATO". *Communist and Post-Communist Studies*, 51:2, 101–111.

Tsygankov, Andrei and Tsygankov, Pavel (2021). "Constructing National Values: the nationally distinctive turn in Russian IR theory and foreign policy". *Foreign Policy Analysis*, 17:4, DOI: https://doi.org/10.1093/fpa/orab022

Umarov, Temur (2021) "Is There a Place for a U.S. Military Base in Central Asia?". *Carnegie Endowment for International Peace*, 4 June 2021, available at https://carnegiemoscow.org/commentary/84685.

Umland, Andreas et al. (2022). "Heavy Weapons Now!" *Krytyka*, July 2022, available at https://krytyka.com/en/articles/heavy-weapons-now, accessed 3 August 2022.

Van Fraassen, Bas C. (1980). *The Scientific Image*. Oxford: Clarendon.

Vershinin, Alex (2022) "The Return of Industrial Warfare". *RUSI (Royal United Services Institute) Commentary*, 17 June 2022, available at https://rusi.org/explore-our-research/publications/commentary/return-industrial-warfare.

Walt, Steven (2022). "The West is Sleepwalking into War in Ukraine". *Foreign Policy*, 23 February 2022, available at https://foreignpolicy.com/2022/02/23/united-states-europe-war-russia-ukraine-sleepwalking/, accessed 17 March 2022.

Waltz, Kenneth (1959). *Man, the State, and War: A Theoretical Analysis*. New York: Columbia University Press.

Walzer, Michael (2006). *Just and Unjust Wars. A Moral Argument with Historical Illustrations*. 4th edition. New York: Basic Books.

Weber, Isabella (2021). *How China Escaped Shock Therapy. The Market Reform Debate*. London and New York: Routledge.

Wendt, Alexander (1999). *Social Theory of International Politics*. Cambridge: Cambridge University Press.

Wendt, Alexander (2003). "Why a World State is Inevitable". *European Journal of International Relations*, 9:4, 491–542.

Wendt, Alexander (2015). *Quantum Mind and Social Science. Unifying Physical and Social Ontology*. Cambridge: Cambridge University Press.

Wikipedia (2022): "Julian Assange", *Wikipedia*, 15 March 2022, available at https://en.wikipedia.org/w/index.php?title=Julian_Assange&oldid=1077356167, accessed 16.3.2022.

Zartman, William I. (2001) "The Timing of Peace Initiatives: hurting stalemates and ripe moments". *The Global Review of Ethnopolitics*, 1:1, 8–18.

Zygar, Mikhail (2016). *All the Kremlin's Men: Inside the Court of Vladimir Putin*. New York: PublicAffairs.

Index

9/11 4, 22, 55

Afghanistan War 22, 52, 53, 60n2
agency 5, 12
Albania 24
Allen, Robert C. 12
analogies: Winter War 4, 78–79n1; World War I 4; World War II 4, 5–6, 49–50
anarchy 41, 42, 73
Angell, Norman 60n6
Anti-Ballistic Missile (ABM) Treaty 73
Arendt, Hannah 16
Arias, Oscar 74
Armenia 32
Assange, Julian 39, 44n8
assassinations 28
atomism 41, 44n11
austerity politics 35
authoritarianism 78: global financial crisis 25; neoliberalisation 34; Russia 11, 14, 25, 31, 38, 71
autocracy 78

Baker, James 8
Baltic states 7, 8
Belarus 23, 32, 33, 52
Berlin, Isaiah 59
best-case scenario 64–65
Bhaskar, Roy 59
Biden, Joe 34, 48, 52, 73
British Empire 55
Brzezinski, Zbigniew 11
Budapest Memorandum 9, 50
Bulgaria 6
Burns, William 17
Bush, George W. 4, 15, 22, 55, 73

Cafruny, Alan 29n1, 43n7
Central America 37
Central Asia 36
certainty-of-hindsight bias *see* hindsight bias
Charter on Strategic Partnership 47
Chechnya 24, 27, 28
chemical weapons 39, 51
Chernomyrdin, Viktor 19n5
China: development 13; future 72; Industrial Revolution counterfactual 2; Iraq War 22; nuclear weapons 73; socio-economic developments 14; UN veto powers 15; US overseas military bases 43n4; weaponisation of interdependence 65; world order 69
Chomsky, Noam 79n2
Clark, Christopher 6n2
climate change 66, 77
Clinton, Bill 7, 15
coercive diplomacy 47, 58
Cold War: end of 4, 7, 9, 13, 16, 21, 36, 44n8, 69, 75; European security order 8; Finland 33, 37; "Finlandisation" 33; new 67–68, 71, 76; Sweden 37; US interests in Central America 37; US interventions 44n8; world politics analysed through prism of 58

colour revolutions 5, 23, 25, 28, 52; Georgia 23–24; Ukraine 23–24, 26, 51
Contact Group on the former Yugoslavia 9, 11
containment 68, 71–72
contrast space 2–3, 19n3
contrastive explanations 1–6
coronavirus pandemic 48, 53, 54
corruption: Russia 21, 29; Ukraine 31, 32, 33, 37, 47, 52, 53
counterfactuals (general discussion) 1–6
Crimea: annexation 5, 12, 31, 32, 34, 38, 46, 52, 61; forum 47, 57; future 62; NATO 36; return to Ukraine, calls for 47, 53, 56; Russian military base 51; US military base, potential 36; water supply cut off 48
Croatia 24
Cuban missile crisis 37, 50, 72
Czech Republic 14
Czechoslovakia 17

de-escalation of war 64, 66, 74
deterrence 66, 68
Deudney, Daniel 73
Deutsch, Karl W. 43n6, 76
disarmament 76
double standards 27, 28, 37, 39, 54

East Central Europe 7, 16
East Germany 8
Eastern Europe: missile defence 30n2; NATO 29n1, 49; World War II 6
end of history 14, 25
escalation of war 65–67, 69–71
essentialism 16, 17, 18, 28, 54
ethical issues 4, 40, 54, 63, 64, 69
euro crisis 34, 35, 38–39, 44n9
Euromaidan protests 31–32, 35, 36, 38–39
EuroMemo Group 44n9
European security order 7–9, 14–15, 18, 29n1, 32
European Union (EU): association agreement 31, 32, 35; build-up to Ukraine War 47, 55; colour revolutions 23; Constitution 44n9; constitutive principles 38; economic developments 17; euro crisis 34, 35, 38–39, 44n9; expansion 25; forces of change 39; future 70, 72; government expenditure 22; Greece's situation 38; influence, methods of 44n8; membership, vs Russia's dominance 37; military force 14; modernisation partnership with the US 27; national characteristics 28; neighbourhood programme 35; neoliberalism 22; Russia's relationship with 16, 21, 25, 38; Transnistrian conflict 26; Ukraine crisis (2013–2014) 31, 32, 33, 38–39; Ukraine's development, attempts to influence 35

far-right groups 53; *see also* populism
financialisation 20n6
Finland: Cold War 33, 37; GDP 70; inequality levels 14; public sector expenditure 22; trade with Soviet Union 45n13; Winter War 4, 78–79n1; World War II 6
First World War *see* World War I
food supply 69, 71
France: build-up to Ukraine War 57; disinformation 60n4; empire 55; European Constitution referendum 44n9; Iraq War 22, 26; Minsk II agreement 48; NATO 27; Revolution 42; UN veto powers 15

G-7 9
Gaddafi, Muammar 27
Garfinkel, Alan 4
gas and oil 12, 21, 46
General Agreement on Tariffs and Trade (GATT) 38
geohistorical layers *see* layers of history
Georgia: NATO 5, 24, 25, 27; Rose Revolution 23–24; Russian "peacekeeping" 9; Russo-Georgian War 24, 27, 34
Germany: build-up to Ukraine War 57; European security order 8; industrial production 14;

international norms 40; Iraq War 26; Minsk II agreement 48; NATO 27; unification 8, 16, 17; Winter War 78–79n1; World War II 2, 4, 51
glasnost 12
global financial crisis 25, 34–35, 39, 75
globalisation 14, 35, 36, 37
good faith in negotiations 51, 56, 58, 60n4
Gorbachev, Mikhail 8, 12
Gore, Al 4
Granoff, Jonathan 74
Great Depression 4
Greece 35, 38
groupthink 54, 60n5

Harvey, Frank 4
Hegel, G.H.F. 42
Herwig, Holger 2
hindsight bias 2, 49, 56, 58
historical nodal points *see* nodal points of history
Hitler, Adolf 2, 4
holism 45n11
human rights 24, 28, 35, 37, 38, 43n2; violations 39
Hungary 17

immediate/proximate causes of war 3, 7, 15
India 69, 72
individualism 40, 41, 44–45n11
Industrial Revolution 2
information operations 34
intermediate causes of war 3
Intermediate-Range Nuclear Forces (INF) Treaty 73, 75
International Court of Justice 51
International Criminal Court 41
International Monetary Fund (IMF) 17, 35
International Relations 3, 25, 45nn11–12
Iraq War 22, 26–27, 28, 58; counterfactual analysis 4; disinformation 60n4; irrationality 60n6; multipolarity principle 25; norm violations 39, 40

Islamic terrorism 22
Ivashov, Leonid 12

Japan 12, 75
Jervis, Robert 70

Kant, Immanuel 42
Kazakhstan 33
Keal, Paul 36
Kekkonen, Urho 37
KGB 11
Khodorkovsky, Mikhail 28, 29
Kirill, Patriarch 53
Kissinger, Henry 79n2
Kosovo 38
Kosovo War 21, 58; disinformation 60n4; European security order 9, 17; multipolarity principle 25; Russian humiliation 10–11
Krause, Joachim 64

layers of history 5, 16, 54
Lebed, Alexander 11
Libyan intervention 27, 40, 58
Litvinenko, Alexander 28
Lukashenko, Alexander 33, 37

market economy 13, 23, 24, 35, 38, 43n2
Mearsheimer, John 9, 33, 35, 42–43nn1–2
Medvedev, Dmitri 27, 50
methodological nationalism/ globalism 45n11
Middle East 71, 72
Milosevic, Slobodan 58
Minsk agreement 46, 47, 48, 54, 57
Minsk II agreement 46, 48, 55, 56
Moldova 26, 33
Molotov–Ribbentrop pact 4
Monroe, James 36, 43n3
Monroe Doctrine 36, 37, 40, 47
Moroccan crisis (1911) 5
Munich agreement 4
mutually hurting stalemate 67, 70

nationalism: EuroMemo Group 44n9; global financial crisis 25; methodological 45n11;

neoliberalisation 34; Russia 4, 11, 22, 25, 71; Ukraine 39, 51

NATO: Bucharest summit (2008) 24, 27; build-up to Ukraine War 47–57; colour revolutions 23; dissolution counterfactual 21, 29n1; expansion 5–10, 15–17, 22, 24–25, 28, 29–30n1, 39, 51, 52, 54, 72; future 65; Georgia 5, 24, 25, 27; intentions as perceived by Russia 43n2; Kosovo War 17, 20n6; Libyan intervention 27; Membership Action Plan 27, 52; membership, vs Russia's dominance 37; military support for Ukraine 63–64; nuclear strategy 65, 75; and OSCE, choice between 29n1; partnership programme 9; Russia as permanent outsider 25; Russia as potential member 8, 15, 16, 22; Ukraine as potential member 5, 24–25, 27, 39, 46–47, 51–53, 55–56, 60n3; US leadership 15, 77

Navalny, Aleksey 34, 44n8

Nazism 51, 59, 78–79n1

neo-imperialism 22–23, 33, 52–53, 55, 73, 75

neoliberalism 13, 16, 34, 35; EU initiatives 35; hegemony 14; oligarchs 29; Russia 22, 24, 29; universalising programme 24

neorealism 45n11

neo-revisionism 24, 71

Netherlands 44n9

New START (Strategic Arms Reduction Treaty) 73

nodal points of history 1, 21; Bush administration (2001–2005) 22–23; colour revolutions 23; Crimea's annexation 34; eastern Ukraine war (2014) 34; global financial crisis 25; Iraq War 22, 25; Putin's first vs second terms 25–26; Ukrainian crisis (2013–2014) 34

Non-Proliferation of Nuclear Weapons Treaty (NPT) 73, 74

North Africa 71

North Atlantic Treaty Organization *see* NATO

nuclear weapons/war: Budapest Memorandum 9; containment 71; future 62, 65–68, 72–76; Iraq War 39; NATO 15; Ukraine 43n1, 51; US 37; Wells's anticipation of 5; World War II counterfactual 2

oil and gas 12, 21, 46

oligarchs 13, 14, 29; financialisation 20n6; Khodorkovsky 28, 29; Putin's agreement with 21

organised crime 13

Organization for Security and Co-operation in Europe (OSCE): Budapest conference (1994) 16; build-up to Ukraine War 47; as central security forum 17; *Charter of Paris for a New Europe* 8, 18n1; Donbas conflict 47; *Istanbul Charter for European Security* 18n1; and NATO, choice between 29n1; and prevention of war 7, 14–15; Russia's status in 15, 77; Ukraine's Orange Revolution 26

O'Rourke, Lindsay 40

Orwell, George, *Nineteen Eighty-Four* 77

OSCE *see* Organization for Security and Co-operation in Europe

peace: prospects for 61–62, 64–67, 69, 75–78; research 3

Peloponnesian War 6n1

perestroika 12

Peter the Great 53

Poland 7, 17

politics and violence 64–65, 76

populism 34, 78: build-up to Ukraine War 53; EuroMemo Group 44n9; Russia 71; Ukraine 39

Pottering, Hans-Gert 19n5

poverty: Russia 13, 21; Ukraine 35

precautionary principle 66

processual social theories 19n4

Prohibition of Nuclear Weapons Treaty 74

prospect theory 53–54

proximate/immediate causes of war 3, 7, 15

Putin, Vladimir: assassinations ordered by 38; authoritarianism 31; Berlin speech (2001) 25–26; build-up to war 46–56, 58, 60n5; colour revolutions 26; election (2000) 21; European security order 8; first vs second terms as nodal point 25–26; future 61, 62, 64, 67, 68, 74; Iraq War 23, 26; Kosovo War 20n6; Mearsheimer on 42n1; Munich speech (2007) 26; nuclear deterrence 72; and oligarchs 21, 28, 29; ousting 38, 52; as person and leader 7, 11–12, 16, 38, 39, 54; popularity 68; prospect theory 60n3; re-election (2012) 31, 52–53; rise 5, 10, 21, 24; sanctions 33; securitisation 24; summit with Biden (June 2021) 48; World War II analogies 4

quantum social theories 19n4

Reagan, Ronald 13
refugee crisis 34
Russia: anti-government protests 31, 36, 39; Beslan terrorist attack (2004) 27; build-up to war 46–58; colour revolutions 23–24, 28; constitutional crisis (1993) 10; Contact Group on the former Yugoslavia 9, 11; counterfactuals and contrastive explanations 4–5; crime 21; Crimea *see* Crimea; democratisation failure 7, 10; economic development (1990s) 10, 12–13, 17, 18; economic development (2000s) 21, 24, 26; European security order 7–9; and EU, relationship between 16, 21, 25, 38; foreign policy (2000s) 25, 26, 28; future 61–75, 77–78; Georgian War 24, 27, 34; global security system 37; government expenditure 22; grand strategy 43n7; humiliation 4, 10–11, 14, 16, 26, 56, 57–58, 77; individualism 40–41; Iraq War 22, 23, 25, 26–27; Kosovo War 10–11; Libyan intervention 27; media 10, 28, 50–51, 58; Moscow terrorist attack (2002) 27; national characteristics 28, 41; national self-esteem 9; nationalism 4; NATO, expansion 7–8, 15, 16, 17, 24, 27; NATO, perceived intentions 43n2; NATO, Russia as permanent outsider 25; NATO, Russia as potential member 8, 15, 16, 22; neo-imperialism 33, 52–53, 55; neoliberalism 22, 24, 29; neo-revisionism 24; norm violations 39–40; OSCE 7, 15; Putin's first vs second terms as nodal point 25–26; Putin's project 21–22; regime change 68, 72; relationship with the West (2010s) 33–34; repositioning (2000s) 25; sanctions 33–34, 65, 71–72, 77; Second Chechen War 27; securitisation 24; securocracy 28; shock therapy 13, 14; spheres of influence 26, 31–33, 36, 40, 41, 42n1; territorial change 9–10; Ukraine's development, attempts to influence 35; Ukrainian crisis (2013–2014) 31–32, 42n1; UN veto powers 15; US overseas military bases 43n4; weakening position in world economy 46; weaponisation of interdependence 65; Western aspirations 38; Winter War analogies 4, 78–79n1; World War II analogies 4, 5–6, 49–50
"Russia first" policy 9
Russo-Georgian War 24, 27, 34

Sachs, Jeffrey 13, 79n2
Sakwa, Richard 71
sanctions 33–34, 65, 71–72, 77
Sanders, Bernie 39
Schmitt, Carl 42
Scholz, Olaf 50
Second Chechen War 24, 27
Second World War *see* World War II
securitisation 23–24, 29, 35, 36, 38
securocracy 28
Shevardnadze, Eduard 17
Shifrinson, Joshua 40
shock therapy 13, 14, 17
siloviks 28

sleepwalking metaphor 4
Slovakia 14
Slovenia 14
social constructivism 45n11
social structures and mechanisms 5
Solana, Javier 26
Soviet Union/former Soviet Union: Cold War, end of 75; collapse 5, 8–12, 14; continuation counterfactual 13; European security order 8, 9; NATO expansion 17; neo-imperialism 52; nostalgia for 55; shock therapy 17; spheres of interest 36; territorial change 9–10; Winter War 4, 78–79n1; world economy 41; World War II 51
spheres of influence/interest 26, 31–33, 36, 40, 41, 42n1
stalemate, mutually hurting 67, 70
Stalin, Joseph 78n1
Stiglitz, Joseph 13
structuration 16
Sweden 37, 44n8
SWIFT 72, 77

Taiwan 69
Tajikistan 9, 43n4
tax havens 20n6
taxation 22
Tetlock, Philip 56, 62, 63
Thatcher, Margaret 13
Thucydides, *Peloponnesian War* 6nn1, 3
Transnistria 9, 26
Treaty on the Conventional Armed Forces in Europe 30n2
Trump, Donald: character 58; and the EU 39; nuclear weapons 73, 74, 75; West–Russia relationship 33, 34
Tsygankov, Andrei and Pavel 25
Turkey 74

Ukraine: Bucha massacre and atrocities 61, 65; Budapest Memorandum 9; build-up to war 46–58; counterfactuals and contrastive explanations 4–5; Crimea *see* Crimea; crisis (2013–2014) 5, 31–32, 34, 38–39; divisions 37; Donbas 46, 47, 51; Donetsk 47; east Ukraine war (2014) 5, 31, 32, 34; economic development 21, 34–35; "Finlandised" 32–33; future 61–74, 78; genocide claims 51; independence 11; language issues 39; Luhansk 47; Maidan protest movement 31–32; military capabilities 47, 52, 53, 56, 57, 63–64, 67, 70; NATO potential membership 5, 24–25, 27, 39, 46–47, 51–53, 55–56, 60n3; Orange Revolution 23–24, 26, 51; spheres of influence 40; Winter War analogies 4; World War I analogies 4; World War II analogies 5–6
ultimate/underlying causes of war 3, 5
underlying/ultimate causes of war 3, 5
Union of Soviet Socialist Republics *see* Soviet Union/former Soviet Union
United Kingdom: disinformation 60n4; Iraq War 22, 25, 28; naval armament 23; UN veto powers 15
United Nations (UN): Charter 69; condemnation of Russia's invasion of Ukraine 69; European security order 9; international law 38; Iraq War 22, 25; Kosovo War 20n6, 21; Libyan intervention 27; military assistance 70; and prevention of war 14–15; Russia's privileged position 15; veto powers 15, 77
United Russia 21–22
United States: 9/11 4, 22, 55; Afghanistan withdrawal 52, 53; Assange 40; build-up to Ukraine War 47–49, 51–53, 55, 58; Bush administration (2001–2005) 22–23; Cold War, violent interventions during 44n8; colour revolutions 23; Contact Group on the former Yugoslavia 9; disinformation 60n4; domestic politics 68; economic developments 17; and the EU, relationship between 27, 39; future 65, 69, 72–74; geopolitical interests and vision 35–36; Grand Strategy

25, 37, 38, 43n7; hegemony 22, 25, 41; Iraq War 22, 25, 26, 28; Islamic terrorism threat 22; Maidan protest movement 31; military aid to Ukraine 48, 52; military bases overseas 36; military force 14; military-industrial complex 29n1; Monroe Doctrine 36, 37, 40, 47; national characteristics 28; National Security Strategy 23; NATO, expansion 7, 8, 15, 27, 29n1; NATO, leadership 15, 77; NATO, Russia's potential membership 22; neo-imperialism 22–23; norm violations 39, 40; nuclear weapons 37, 73, 74, 75; "reset" policy 27; rule of law 41; Russian individualism 41; Soviet Union's collapse 14; spheres of influence/interest 36, 41; Ukraine's development, attempts to influence 35; UN veto powers 15; war on terror 24; World War II counterfactual 2
Unity 21
universal monarchy/dictatorship 41–42

Versailles peace treaty 4
violence and politics 64–65, 76
Visegrad countries 17
Voronin, Vladimir 26

Waltz, Kenneth 7
Walzer, Michael 70
war crimes 62
war on terror 24

war reparations 62
Warsaw Pact 16
weaponisation of interdependence 65
Wells, H.G., *The World Set Free* 5
Wendt, Alexander 42
"Westsplaining" 66–67, 70
"whataboutism" 26, 28, 38, 39, 40, 41
Winter War 4, 78–79n1
world economy 46
world order 68, 69, 71
world time 19–20n6, 41
World Trade Organization (WTO) 38
World War I 3–4, 5
World War II: aftermath 68; analogies with Ukraine War 4, 5–6, 49–50; counterfactual analysis 2; Germany's surprise attack on Soviet Union 51; normatively loaded language 59; nuclear weapons 75; Operation Barbarossa 17; spheres of influence 36
worst-case scenario 64, 65–66

Yandarbiyev, Zelimkhan 28
Yanukovych, Viktor 26, 31, 32, 39
Yeltsin, Boris: drunkenness 11; European security order 8; hegemony 14; NATO expansion 16; neoliberalism 22; potential successors 11; shock therapy 17
Yugoslavia 10, 58; Contact Group on the former 9, 11; *see also* Kosovo War
Yushchenko, Viktor 26

Zelenskyy, Volodymyr 47, 52

For Product Safety Concerns and Information please contact our EU
representative GPSR@taylorandfrancis.com
Taylor & Francis Verlag GmbH, Kaufingerstraße 24, 80331 München, Germany

www.ingramcontent.com/pod-product-compliance
Lightning Source LLC
Chambersburg PA
CBHW051757230426
43670CB00012B/2324